THE WAR RECORD

OF THE

1/5th (Earl of Chester's) Battalion

The Cheshire Regiment.

Lieut.-Col. J. E. G. Groves, C.M.G., T.D.

THE War Record

OF THE

1/5th (Earl of Chester's) Battalion The Cheshire Regiment,

August, 1914——June, 1919.

BY

Lieut.-Col. W. A. V. Churton, D.S.O., T.D.

The Naval & Military Press Ltd

Reproduced by kind permission of the Central Library,
Royal Military Academy, Sandhurst

Published by
The Naval & Military Press Ltd
Unit 10 Ridgewood Industrial Park,
Uckfield, East Sussex,
TN22 5QE England
Tel: +44 (0) 1825 749494
Fax: +44 (0) 1825 765701
www.naval-military-press.com
www.military-genealogy.com
www.militarymaproom.com

In reprinting in facsimile from the original, any imperfections are inevitably reproduced and the quality may fall short of modern type and cartographic standards.

PREFACE.

In response to a frequently expressed desire, that a history of the 1/5th (Earl of Chester's) Battalion the Cheshire Regiment should be written, I have endeavoured in the following pages to give a concise record of the Battalion's work during the War, from 1914 to 1919 in England, France and Flanders.

In a War of such magnitude as the late War the doings of a single Battalion counted for little. The Division, being composed of all arms, was generally the Unit which fought, and I have considered it necessary in order that the Battalion's share in active operations may be made intelligible and viewed in the right light, in several cases to go beyond mere details of the Battalion's work and to describe generally the operations of the Corps and Divisions to which it was attached.

My aim has been to give an accurate account of facts, and not to introduce any elements of fiction. My efforts in this direction have been greatly facilitated by having access to the official War Diary of the Battalion, and to a large number of original messages and orders, many of which were kindly lent me by various officers of the Unit. The records of casualties have all been most carefully checked and are compiled from the official lists. No doubt mistakes and omissions have been made, but I feel sure that any reader who discovers these will "Have me excused."

In 1914, the title of the Unit was the 5th Battalion and the following is the reason why it was changed to that of the 1/5th Battalion.

At the outbreak of War the 1st and 2nd Battalions of the Cheshire Regiment were Regular Battalions, the 3rd Battalion was a Special Reserve Battalion, and the 4th, 5th, 6th and 7th Battalions were all Territorial Battalions. Very shortly after mobilization in August, 1914, owing to the rush of recruits, second line units of all the Territorial Battalions were formed, and in September, 1914, a new 5th (Reserve) Battalion was created to which all recruits for the 5th Battalion were posted. These recruits were trained at Chester and as they became efficient were drafted to the 5th Battalion. In January, 1915, the title of the 5th Battalion was changed to the 1/5th Battalion, and the 5th (Reserve) Battalion was renamed the 2/5th Battalion the Cheshire Regiment. On the 1/5th Battalion's departure for France in February, 1915, the 2/5th Battalion was moved to Cambridge and became a separate and independent Unit instead of a draft-finding one, being then under the command of Lieut.-Colonel D. Abercromby. During the whole War the 2/5th Battalion was employed as a complete Unit for home defence being stationed on the East Coast. In March, 1915, a further Battalion was formed and called the 3/5th Battalion. This Battalion trained its recruits at Chester and subsequently moved to Oswestry. This Unit furnished drafts for the 1/5th Battalion abroad and acted as its home or depot Battalion, being the Unit which officers and men of the 1/5th Battalion who had been sent home from Foreign Service sick or wounded, after recovery rejoined. This 3rd line was in

August, 1916, amalgamated with the 3rd lines of the 4th, 6th and 7th Battalions of the Regiment and was renamed the 4th (Reserve) Battalion the Cheshire Regiment.

Owing to the strict censorship regulations which forbade the use of cameras in the war zone, it has been impossible to publish any photographs other than official ones, except those taken after the armistice. The War Office authorities very kindly gave me permission to publish official maps and extracts from them, and rendered me great help and assistance by supplying me with copies of the necessary trench maps. My thanks are also due to Mr. Mark Cook, Photographer, of Chester, for his kindness in allowing me to publish certain photographs taken by him. I am also greatly indebted to all the officers of the Battalion who furnished me with invaluable data on innumerable subjects, and especially to Colonel J. E. G. Groves, C.M.G., T.D., for the loan of a large number of original letters, documents and maps which have been of the utmost value in ensuring the accuracy of the details of the various operations described. My warmest appreciative thanks must be expressed to Captain N. B. Ellington, M.C., who took exceptional pains to assist me in revising and correcting proofs, made invaluable suggestions, and was always a willing and safe authority to be referred to when any doubt arose as to the accuracy of detail.

W. A. V. C.

CONTENTS.

		PAGE
Chapter I. 1914. Mobilization and Training in England	... ...	1
„ II. 1915. With 5th Division—Neuve Eglise, Kemmel, Ypres, Vaux, Maricourt, Bray	... ...	24
„ III. 1916. With 56th Division—Gommecourt, Somme, Laventie		44
„ IV. 1917. „ „ Arras, Ypres, Cambrai	...	63
„ V. 1918. „ „ Arras, Croisilles, Canal du Nord, Armistice	... ...	75
„ VI. After the Armistice, Demobilization. Return of Cadre to England	... ...	93
„ VII. Conclusion	... ...	101
Honours and Awards	... ...	105
Record of Officers' Service Abroad	... ...	108
Roll of Officers who Served Overseas with the Battalion	... ...	111
Location Table of Head Quarters	... ...	117
Roll of Honour	... .	121
Summary of Casualties	... ...	130

MAPS.

		PAGE
1.	Trenches in front of Neuve Eglise	27
2.	Kemmel Trenches and Approaches	29
3.	No. 27 and 28 Trenches, Ypres, and Approaches	31
4.	No. 28 Trench, Ypres	33
5.	Vaux Sur Somme	36
6.	Trenches in front of Maricourt	38
7.	Attack at Gommecourt	49
8.	Gropi Trench	57
9.	Leuze Wood Trenches, Somme	57
10.	1st Battle of Arras	65
11.	Trench System held by 56th Division, May to July, 1917	67
12.	Battle of Cambrai	72
13.	Trench System held by 56th Division, January to March, 1918	77
14.	,, ,, ,, April to July, 1918	81
15.	Attack on Canal du Nord	87
16.	Final Advance towards Mons	89

CHAPTER I.

1914.

Mobilization and Training in England.

THE 5th (Earl of Chester's) Battalion, the Cheshire Regiment, was formed from the old 2nd and 3rd Volunteer Battalions, on the Territorial Force scheme of 1908 coming into operation. In 1914 it was under the command of Lieut.-Colonel J. E. G. Groves, T.D., and carried out its annual training at Rhyl, at Whitsuntide. The Battalion formed part of the Cheshire Infantry Brigade, which was composed of the 4th, 5th, 6th, and 7th Battalions of the Cheshire Regiment, under the command of Brigadier-General Cowans, with Capt. A. C. Crookenden as his Brigade Major, and was one of the three Infantry Brigades of the Welsh Division. The area from which the Battalion was recruited was rather scattered. Head Quarters were stationed at Chester, which also furnished " B " and " E " Companies, under the respective commands of Capt. W. A. V. Churton and Capt. A. J. Musgrave. The other Companies and their commanders were :—" A " Company, Hale and Knutsford, Captain G. Hatt Cook ; " C " Company, Sale and Cheadle, Captain H. Watts ; " D " Company, Northwich, Hartford and Kelsall, Captain E. D. Dickson ; " F " Company, Frodsham and Lymm, Lieutenant N. B. Ellington ; " G " Company, Runcorn, Captain Weissmuller ; and " H " Company, Northwich, Lieut. G. H. Brunner. The Adjutant of the Battalion was Captain G. Adshead. The Battalion was armed with the long Lee Enfield rifle and equipped with the Mills web equipment without valises. There were also, at

Chester, a Machine Gun Section, recruited from the Hydraulic Engineering Company, with two Maxims, and a Signal Section. No transport was in the possession of the Unit, nor was there any personnel trained in transport duties.

A scheme for mobilization had been carefully prepared in great detail some time previously to mobilization, and this had been kept thoroughly up-to-date, so that when the word "Mobilize" was wired to Head Quarters at 6 p.m. on August 4th, 1914, the well-oiled machinery was at once set working. Telegrams were sent to all the Company Head Quarters, posters printed in readiness beforehand, were put up on pre-arranged sites, officers on the reserve were called up, and the men all flocked to their respective Drill Halls, where the hundred and one details of mobilization were rapidly and efficiently carried out. The Drill Halls became perfect hives of industry. Recruits came in in large numbers; boots, shirts, and other clothing were issued; horses, and carts of all shapes and sizes, which had previously been earmarked for the purpose, were collected and brought in, and on the fifth day the Battalion concentrated at Chester at the Skating Rink in Northgate Street, and was ready to move to its War Station at Shrewsbury. The strength of the Battalion was 27 officers and 975 other ranks, which included nine from the Cheshire Brigade A.S.C. for transport duties, four from the 4th Cheshire Regiment attached for Post Office duties, and five from the 1st Welsh Field Ambulance R.A.M.C. (T.F.) for water duties. The following is the composition of the Battalion in detail :—

HEAD QUARTERS.

Lt.-Col. J. E. G. Groves, T.D.	Commanding
Major C. E. Bromley	Second in Command
Capt. G. Adshead	Adjutant
Lieut. S. P. Gamon	Machine Gun Officer
Hon. Capt. and Qmr. T. Dutton	Quartermaster
Lieut. P. T. Warren, R.A.M.C. (T.F.)	Medical Officer.

Regimental Sergt.-Major   J. Kinnest
Regimental Quartermaster Sergt.   W. G. Lockwood
Permanent Staff:—
    Cl. Sergt. A. Sernberg
    Sergt. J. Hall
    Sergt. J. Hamman.

"A" COMPANY.
Capt. G. Hatt-Cook
2nd Lieut. L. Evans
Cl. Sergt. J. W. Wilkinson
153 other Ranks.

"B" COMPANY.
Capt. W. A. V. Churton
Lieut. N. B. Ellington
Cl. Sergt. G. Tilston
131 other Ranks.

"C" COMPANY.
Capt. H. Watts
Lieut. C. A. Price
Lieut. H. Caldecutt
Cl. Sergt. H. Holt
158 other Ranks.

"D" COMPANY.
Capt. E. D. Dickson
Lieut. A. E. Hodgkin
Cl. Sergt. A. Darlington
87 other Ranks.

"E" COMPANY.
Capt. A. J. Musgrave
Lieut. J. H. Davies
2nd Lieut. E. J. Bairstow
Cl. Sergt. F. Weston
141 other Ranks.

"F" COMPANY.
Major T. L. Fennell
Lieut. G. W. C. Hartley
Cl. Sergt. J. Holland
107 other Ranks.

"G" COMPANY.
Capt. R. E. Weissmuller
Lieut. E. S. Bourne
Lieut. A. B. M. Lake
Cl. Sergt. R. Jones
94 other Ranks.

"H" COMPANY.
Capt. J. P. Jackson
Lieut. G. H. Brunner
2nd Lieut. F. A. Freeth (Transport Officer)
75 other Ranks.

At Depôt: 2nd Lieut. W. Vernon.

NOTE.—2nd Lieut. A. Burnett, who was on the strength of the Battalion, was on leave in U.S.A. and rejoined in September.

On August 5th a small party from " E " Company, under Lieut. J. H. Davies, had been sent to act as a guard at the Liverpool Waterworks at Lake Vyrnwy, and on August 8th further orders were suddenly received that one Company was to proceed to Queen's Ferry, Flintshire, to act as a guard over

German Prisoners and interned alien enemy civilians, " B " Company being detailed for this duty. In the early hours of the morning of the 10th, the Battalion (less " B " Company) marched to the General Station and entrained for Shrewsbury, where the Cheshire Brigade and the Welsh Division were concentrating.

A Depôt was now opened for the Battalion at the Drill Hall, Chester, and arrangements were made for the enlistment and training of recruits at the various Drill Halls in the Battalion's area.

On the morning of the 10th, " B " Company, under Capt. W. A. V. Churton, marched to Queen's Ferry where, on arrival, they found that the arrangements for the reception and guarding of the prisoners were in a very backward state. They were later joined by " H " Company, and during their stay there they had plenty of hard work with guard duties, and in erecting barbed wire fences, and generally getting into order the camp, situated in Messrs. Willans and Robinson's disused works, which later in the war became part of the great national explosives factory at Queen's Ferry.

The Commanding Officer had during mobilization asked for volunteers for Foreign Service, and had received a large and gratifying response to his appeal. On arrival at Shrewsbury a further appeal was made to the Brigade, but with only fairly satisfactory results, as sufficient time had not been given to the men for the consideration of such a step at so early a stage in the War. On August 22nd the Battalion marched to Church Stretton, and there " B " and " H " Companies rejoined them at the end of the month, having been relieved by a Company of Royal Welsh Fusiliers.

Whilst at Church Stretton an attempt was made to constitute two composite Battalions from the Brigade, for Foreign Service,

"B" Company during Mobilization at Drill Hall, Chester.

"B" Company leaving Drill Hall, Chester, for Queen's Ferry.

Group of eight Privates who joined the Battalion on the outbreak of War, seven of whom obtained Commissions in the Battalion.

Pte. F. Caress.   Pte. N. Holmstrom.   Pte. H. F. Davies.   Pte. B. S. Walker.
Pte. T. L. C. Heald.   Pte. A. H. Cowap.   Pte. H. N. Hignett.   Pte. H. L. Churton.

by transferring those volunteering from their Units to the Composite Battalions, which were formed on the Establishments of the 5th and 7th Battalions, but the attempt caused so much feeling, and diminished the *espirit de corps* to such an extent, that it was abandoned the following day, to the relief of all concerned.

At the end of August the whole of the Welsh Division moved to Northampton, the Battalion being billeted in the Euston Road area. This area consisted of a number of streets of small houses, in which small parties of from three to six men had comfortable billets. Each Company had certain streets allotted to it, the company officers being billeted in the same street as their men. The supply of meals presented some little difficulty at first, but a system was soon adopted whereby the cooking and rapid distribution of the food was effected. Baths were arranged for the men at the Corporation Swimming Baths. Owing to the scattered nature of the billets, no Battalion Officers' Mess was practicable, but the Officers dined together one night in each week at the Plough Hotel, which was Battalion Head Quarters. Very shortly after arrival, all ranks were inoculated against enteric fever. Serious training was at once commenced. The work was hard but progressive, and all ranks soon began to get fit and excellent progress made towards efficiency.

At the commencement, training was under company arrangements, and later a thorough course of Battalion training was gone through. The programme for each week included a Brigade route march, which was carried out in full marching order under the strictest march discipline, under the keen supervision of the Brigade Major, the length of each march being gradually increased up to a maximum of fifteen miles.

The Battalion, after completing its Battalion training, underwent a more advanced course of Brigade Battle training, under the Brigadier; during this period a divisional route march of twelve miles was carried out with full transport, the occasion being noteworthy owing to the fact that the leading troops of the column were returning to the town, having completed their march, before the last ones had left, due to the great length of a division in Battle order in column of route.

On October 31st the Battalion moved by train to Needham Market and marched to Coddenham, Suffolk, where it went into billets. The cause of their moving to this area was the necessity of constructing trenches for the defence of the East Coast, and some very strenuous work was put in here on ground that was very wet and unsuitable for trench work.

In the early part of November orders were received for the Division to proceed to India, and the Battalion returned to Northampton to equip, and leave was granted to the men; but the orders were very soon cancelled and fresh orders were received to move to the East Coast again, to continue on the Scheme of Defence; and at the beginning of December the Battalion once again moved to Suffolk, to Stowmarket, to carry on with further work in digging trenches. Whilst in this town the Battalion passed their first Christmas together, which was kept in time-honoured style by a series of entertainments and Company dinners, consisting of turkey and plum pudding. The turkeys were easily obtained in this part of the country famed for turkeys, and the puddings were provided by the kindness of the ladies of Stowmarket, who were indefatigable in their efforts to make the day a success.

In November three Battalions from the Division, the 6th Cheshires, the 4th Royal Welsh Fusiliers, and the 2nd Monmouth Regiment, had proceeded to France, and it soon became known that the 5th Battalion was next on the list for the same destination.

At the beginning of January orders were received for the Battalion to move to Cambridge, to equip for Foreign Service. On their arrival, Battalion Head Quarters were established in Magdalene College, the rest of the Battalion being billeted in Chesterton.

During the period of the Battalion's training, a large number of recruits had joined at the several drill halls and undergone a course of recruits training. A large draft of these had recently joined the Unit and were awaiting them at Cambridge.

As the establishment of the Battalion for Foreign Service had to be 1,000 rank and file, it became necessary to recruit the Battalion, which had been reduced by men having been passed unfit for service abroad, up to this strength, and volunteers were asked for from the 4th and 7th Battalions of the Regiment. There was no difficulty in obtaining these, men eagerly coming forward, the 7th Cheshires furnishing 211, and 4th Cheshires 90 men, so that the War Strength of 30 Officers and 1,000 men was quickly reached.

The Battalion was now ordered, on short notice, to re-organize on a double Company Basis, and to carry this out " A " and " C " Companies were amalgamated under Major Watts, " B " and " E " under Captain W. A. V. Churton, " F " and " G " under Captain C. A. Price, and " D " and " H " under Captain N. B. Ellington. Training was carried out daily, and fresh equipment and stores were issued. The transport was entirely re-organized, a large number of mules being taken over in place of horses already in possession, and a completely new set of transport vehicles was provided. All the rifles in the possession of the Unit had also to be altered in order to take the new ammunition with the pointed bullet. Web equipment was issued to all Officers, who discarded their Sam Browne equipment and swords, so that every Officer was equipped exactly the same as a man with the exception that he carried a revolver instead of a rifle and bayonet. Officers valises were rigorously cut down to the regulation 35 lbs. Whilst at Cambridge the Welsh Division was reviewed by His Majesty King George V. on Parker's Piece. The Battalion took part in the parade and was inspected by His Majesty and subsequently marched past in double column of fours.

At the beginning of February orders were received for the Battalion to proceed overseas for service, and on February 14th the Battalion left Cambridge. The constitution of the Battalion then was as follows :—

HEAD QUARTERS.

Commanding Officer	Lt.-Col. J. E. G. Groves, T.D.
Second in Command	Major T. L. Fennell
Adjutant	Captain J. H. Davies
Machine Gun Officer	Lieutenant S. P. Gamon
Quartermaster	Captain T. Dutton
Medical Officer	Lieutenant W. Rogers, R.A.M.C.
Regimental Sergt.-Major	J. Kinnest
Regimental Quartermaster Sergt.	H. Holt.

"A" COMPANY.

Major H. Watts
Captain F. A. Freeth
Lieutenant A. Burnett (T.O.)
        „   S. H. Smith
        „   O. Johnson
        „   H. N. Hignett.

531	A/C.S.M.	Corbett, E. A.	578	L/Sergt.	Drake, C.
17	C.Q.M.S.	Carson, H. R.	1197	„	Norbury, F.
11	Sergeant	Cash, T.	777	Corporal	Newall, W. H.
625	„	Goodier, J.	1125	„	Trelfa, N. E.
1576	„	Whitehead, T.	1285	A/Corpl.	Southern, S. H.
89	„	Maddocks, G. T.	1244	„	Boardman, E.
745	„	Fletcher, R.	1710	„	Raynor, W.
98	„	Dutton, T.	419	„	Percival, R. N.
1	„	Wilkinson, J. W.	1356	„	Southwell, A.
1815	A/Sergt.	White, W.	354	„	Bradley, A.

"A" Company—Continued.

1245	L/Corpl.	Epplestone, W.	1869	Private	Comer, R. L.
2057	,,	Lanceley, H.	1398	,,	Champion, A. L.
1711	,,	Robinson, J.	1712	,,	Cash, Alf.
1573	,,	Jones, A.	1634	,,	Cash, H.
1354	,,	Radcliffe, B.	1629	,,	Cash, F.
1505	,,	Glover, C.	1628	,,	Cash, A.
1409	,,	Wright, J.	2012	,,	Cook, P.
1734	,,	Bywater, F. G.	2104	,,	Crowther, H.
1345	,,	Armstrong, E.	1376	,,	Coombes, J.
2451	,,	Ridings, W. J.	2028	,,	Chapman, G. B.
1343	,,	Ackerley, C.	2145	,,	Chapman, J.
1619	Drummer	Blackshaw, H.	1527	,,	Clifford, J.
1727	,,	Clarkson, W.	1894	,,	Dixon, T. F.
1728	,,	Sutcliffe, H.	1755	,,	Dawson, F.
1668	,,	Worthington, T.	1703	,,	Davidson, B. W.
1891	Private	Allen, S.	1549	,,	Day, J.
2043	,,	Abrahams, W.	1757	,,	Daniels, C.
1910	,,	Atkinson, A.	1857	,,	Duffy, T.
1107	,,	Atkinson, C.	1583	,,	Davies, J.
1621	,,	Axon, R.	1913	,,	Dodwell, J. E.
1344	,,	Alsop, S.	2111	,,	Doyle, J.
1578	,,	Allaby, G.	1413	,,	Edge, G.
2116	,,	Armstrong, A. A.	675	,,	Eden, G.
1657	,,	Bicknell, W.	1870	,,	Fox, F.
1512	,,	Bradley, J.	1627	,,	Fletcher, J.
1893	,,	Buchanan, J.	1617	,,	Fletcher, J. W.
2119	,,	Blease, J.	1460	,,	Fletcher, R.
1868	,,	Boardman, J. W.	2055	,,	Foy, A.
1892	,,	Berry, H.	1296	,,	Gallimore, P.
137	,,	Bowker, G.	1547	,,	Groves, W.
51	,,	Bracegirdle, P.	1976	,,	Gilligan, C.
1649	,,	Bracegirdle, G.	1751	,,	Hamnett, N.
1561	,,	Bostock, A.	1441	,,	Holt, J.
1551	,,	Bostock, M.	2095	,,	Holt, E.
1622	,,	Brookes, E.	1397	,,	Hicks, S. R.
1736	,,	Brocklehurst, V.	1939	,,	Hickman, E. G.
1377	,,	Brickell, S.	1572	,,	Hayward, F. C.
1559	,,	Burrows, H.	1552	,,	Haslam, J.
1701	,,	Barton, T.	1967	,,	Hill, H.
2183	,,	Cruckshanks, G.	1940	,,	Hill, G.
1937	,,	Cox, W.	1350	,,	Heaviside, E.
2418	,,	Cleary, H. V.	1584	,,	Hurst, H.
1699	,,	Cameron, W.	755	,,	Heaton, L.
1752	,,	Comar, E.	1597	,,	Hooley, J.

"A" COMPANY—*Continued.*

1596	Private	Jackson, J. H.	2017	Private	Pugh, H.
2096	,,	Jones, W. K.	2121	,,	Roberts, H.
1661	,,	Jones, S.	923	,,	Rawlinson, A. E.
1563	,,	Jones, Alf.	1735	,,	Royle, J.
1917	,,	Jones, T. W.	1920	,,	Rackstraw, W.
1803	,,	Jenkins, N. H.	1599	,,	Renshaw, F.
1871	,,	Knowles, H.	2101	,,	Rooney, G.
2026	,,	Kenyon, E.	1811	,,	Redfern, G.
1979	,,	Kendall, J. A.	2100	,,	Royle, E.
1877	,,	Kitson, J. A.	1426	,,	Sheldon, H.
1461	,,	Kirkland, H.	1664	,,	Speakman, J.
1756	,,	Lamb, C.	2059	,,	Skelhorn, S.
1544	,,	Leigh, H.	1502	,,	Sloan, J.
1445	,,	Marsland, H.	803	,,	Thornber, G.
1442	,,	Macnamara, A.	1357	,,	Townley, J.
1662	,,	Macdonald, G.	593	,,	Vaughan, T.
1352	,,	Massey, L.	1633	,,	Venables, F.
2020	,,	Marsland, R.	1358	,,	Vernon, A.
1816	,,	Morrissy, F.	1748	,,	Vesey, F.
1595	,,	Minshall, J.	1666	,,	Warburton, J.
1942	,,	Neild, H.	2450	,,	Warburton, C.
1802	,,	Nuttall, T. J.	2761	,,	Ward, F.
1464	,,	Ogden, G. H.	1630	,,	Walker, J.
785	,,	Ogden, J.	2090	,,	Wilson, J.
1982	,,	Owens, R. J.	1741	,,	Wildgoose, J. W.
1758	,,	Parsonage, J. H.	1878	,,	Wolfenden, H.
2098	,,	Penny, H.	857	,,	Wilkins, J. H.

MEN ATTACHED FROM 7TH BATTALION.

1826	L/Corpl.	Stanley, H.	1709	Private	Gaunt, A.
54	Private	Beresford, J.	1295	,,	Gibson, G.
1609	,,	Boffey, N.	1851	,,	Goodwin, G.
1854	,,	Betterley, J.	2008	,,	Goodwin, J.
1460	,,	Brown, R. J.	1725	,,	Green, W.
1619	,,	Barnshaw, W.	1844	,,	Galgani, A.
1787	,,	Cope, A.	1788	,,	Hood, T.
1627	,,	Cotterill, J.	305	,,	Hough, J.
1419	,,	Charlesworth, F.	1899	,,	Jackson, W.
1843	,,	Clayton, E.	2055	,,	King, J.
1576	,,	Dimelow, D.	1780	,,	Moss, S.
1557	,,	Davies, J.	1564	,,	Mattimore, L.
1418	,,	Dawson, G.	1399	,,	Mayers, A.
1618	,,	Drabble, J.	1412	,,	Nolan, L.
1630	,,	Frost, C.	1726	,,	Pyatt, J.

MOBILIZATION AND TRAINING IN ENGLAND.

"A" COMPANY—*Continued*.

1827	Private	Rowley, L.	1658	Private	Smart, J.
1856	,,	Roome, H.	1657	,,	Turner, F.
1286	,,	Rotherham, J.	2013	,,	Tomkinson, A.
1463	,,	Stockton, J.	1403	,,	Taylor, J. T.
1715	,,	Stephens, J.	1886	,,	Wood, E.
1958	,,	Stanier, N.	1850	,,	Wright, S.

MEN ATTACHED FROM 4TH BATTALION.

1538	Private	Collins, G.	11	Private	Jones, R.
1233	,,	Croxon, A.	1377	,,	Morris, W. E.
1247	,,	Carter, P. R.	2115	,,	Madden, W.
2083	,,	Ellis, W. S.	1173	,,	Price, A.
2175	,,	Gordon, R. M.	2047	,,	Todd, C.
1415	,,	Goodacre, A. E.	1624	,,	Williams, C.

DRIVERS (1ST LINE TRANSPORT).

1601	Private	Allen, A.	1943	Private	Jones, R.
1859	,,	Moran, F.			

COMPANY BATMEN.

1529	Private	Fisher, J. L.	1919	Private	Lewis, G.
1545	,,	Harrison, J. W.	1918	,,	Robinson, J.
2404	,,	Jones, W. H.			

ATTACHED.

Armourer S. Sergeant		1613	A.S.S.	Marshall, J. H.
Medical Officer's Orderly		1251	Private	Champion, O.

DRIVERS (1ST LINE TRANSPORT).

2013	Private	Dearn, G.	1944	Private	Timperly, W.
1936	,,	Cooper, W.	1964	,,	Benson, E.
1948	,,	Graham, A.	1298	,,	Broome, F.
2024	,,	Pybus, H.	1753	,,	McNealy, R.

HEAD QUARTER'S BATMEN.

1817	Private	Chesters, W. E.	2014	Private	Hollins, J.

PIONEERS.

1169	Sergeant	Watkinson, J. W.	1623	Private	Cash, A.
547	Private	Buckley, C. F.	2127	,,	Newboult, A.

SIGNALLERS.

1658	Private	Britten, J.	1558	Private	Bethel, H.
1896	,,	Hughes, A.	1414	,,	Jackson, F.
1525	,,	Denman, A.			

"A" COMPANY—Continued.

Stretcher Bearers.

1737	Private	Brookes, R.	1882	Private	Jones, H.
1530	,,	Fisher, A. F.	1663	,,	Roberts, J. W.

Machine Gunners.

1782	Private	Brockbank, T.	2011	Private	Clayton, A. E.

Machine Gun Drivers (1st Line Transport).

1705	Private	Kitchen, H.

"B" COMPANY.

Captain W. A. V. Churton
  ,,   H. Caldecutt
Lieutenant E. J. Bairstow
  ,,   L. Evans
2nd Lieut. C. N. Holmstrom
  ,,   T. L. C. Heald.

2113	C.S.M.	Warnock, A.	165	L/Corpl.	Roberts, J. H.
138	A/C.Q.M.S.	Pollard, E. M.	117	,,	Stanton, E. J.
213	Sergeant	Jones, A.	2339	,,	Wadelin, J. T.
693	,,	Wilson, C. A.	2334	,,	Clarke, J. C.
1557	A/Sergt.	Baxter, G. J.	1804	Drummer	Cooper, F.
177	,,	Brooks, S.	1454	,,	Eastham. T.
2176	,,	Harrison, C. R.	1126	,,	Entwistle, H.
2232	,,	Holding, G. H.	1834	,,	Lamb, J.
938	,,	Paulson, H.	2330	Private	Allington, E.
1670	,,	Williamson, J.	1080	,,	Astbury, A.
399	Corporal	Shingler, W.	1326	,,	Astbury, W.
1305	A/Corpl.	Burton, D.	2123	,,	Bailey, J.
2240	,,	Errington, A. E.	2253	,,	Ball, W. J.
1351	,,	Jones, W. O.	2246	,,	Banks, C.
1419	,,	Lamb, A.	1339	,,	Barlow, W.
1435	,,	Street, D.	1480	,,	Barton, J.
1771	,,	Thomas, S.	1329	,,	Biggins, E. H.
2236	,,	Singleton, W. H.	2356	,,	Bostock, R.
995	L/Corpl.	Brierley, B. T.	2562	,,	Bradbury, F.
1677	,,	Evans, J.	1389	,,	Brierley, G. A.
2174	,,	Hewitt, C. G.	1541	,,	Buckley, E.
293	,,	Lewis, R.	2298	,,	Burghall, E.
2233	,,	Paddock, W. H.	1722	,,	Burkhill, T.
1687	,,	Price, T.	2546	,,	Byrne, E. H.

"B" Company—Continued.

2261	Private	Cartwright, J. E.	2072	Private	May, A. G.
2042	,,	Capper, A. E.	2384	,,	Maynard, S.
1988	,,	Catherall, W. E.	1295	,,	Meredith, G.
1538	,,	Chesters, A. E.	1406	,,	Meredith, J. A.
2335	,,	Cook, W. H.	1607	,,	Meredith, T.
2572	,,	Coombs, E.	2181	,,	Mitchell, W.
1532	,,	Davies, A.	2172	,,	Molyneux, G. H.
2175	,,	Davies, P. W.	2305	,,	Naylor, H.
1564	,,	Davies, S. T.	2258	,,	Nicholas, C. E.
1266	,,	Duckers, W. W.	1535	,,	Paddock, C. H.
1832	,,	Dutton, J.	1393	,,	Pagett, W. H.
1534	,,	Feeney, T.	2273	,,	Peers, F.
2413	,,	Gilgrass, A. E.	1874	,,	Pinches, J.
1439	,,	Goff, J.	1556	,,	Plevin, S.
1849	,,	Griffiths, G.	1392	,,	Price, C. L.
2039	,,	Hayes, A. H.	2372	,,	Reddish, A.
1743	,,	Hayter, C. W.	1258	,,	Shallcross, G.
1574	,,	Heath, A.	1718	,,	Sheridan, W.
2251	,,	Heywood, J. L.	1839	,,	Siddall, N.
1337	,,	Hibbert. G.	1960	,,	Simpson, N.
1714	,,	Higginson, A.	1335	,,	Smith, J. E.
1565	,,	Hunt, T. W.	2336	,,	Steventon, R.
1898	,,	Jagger, A.	2262	,,	Stoddard, J. E.
1984	,,	Jones, E.	2329	,,	Stone, J. T.
2208	,,	Jones, E. A.	1537	,,	Stuttard, H. S.
1568	,,	Jones, F. E.	2325	,,	Tasker, F. P.
1821	,,	Jones, J. J.	1334	,,	Thomas, W.
1837	,,	Jones, P.	2403	,,	Thorpe, H.
2462	,,	Jones, S.	2328	,,	Tiddy, P. E.
1394	,,	Jones, W.	1542	,,	Tilston, A.
2078	,,	Jones, R. A.	2205	,,	Walton, J.
2124	,,	Lavender, W.	2122	,,	Warburton, A.
1947	,,	Ledsham, J.	1569	,,	Welford, F. L.
1239	,,	Little, P.	2173	,,	Wilford, H.
1747	,,	Lockley, W.	1808	,,	Williams, G.
1567	,,	Lunn, J. F.	1899	,,	Williams, S.
1328	,,	Malone, H.	2338	,,	Williams, R. R.

Men Attached from 7th Battalion.

317	L/Corpl.	Challinor, J.	1605	Private	Allen, S.
1892	,,	Hay, A. G.	357	,,	Arnold, T.
1022	,,	Wareing, E.	1607	,,	Bailey, C.
1439	Private	Ainsworth. P.	844	,,	Barlow, W.
1794	,,	Alcock, J. T.	1809	,,	Barnes, G.

"B" COMPANY—*Continued.*

1901	Private	Barnett, G.	1270	Private	Hockenhull, R.
1053	,,	Beard, J.	1273	,,	Hulme, G.
2052	,,	Bennett, J.	1915	,,	Hulme, H.
1603	,,	Birtles, A.	1746	,,	Hudson, W. H.
1800	,,	Blackshaw, J.	1590	,,	Hunt, A.
1356	,,	Boulton, G. W.	1538	,,	Justin, H.
1268	,,	Bowyer, R.	1644	,,	Kelly, C.
1549	,,	Braddock, J. W.	2264	,,	Latham, A.
1535	,,	Brierley, S.	809	,,	Malkin, H.
1802	,,	Broughton, R.	1566	,,	Mannion, S.
1829	,,	Brown, J.	1537	,,	Morris, J.
1988	,,	Boulger, J. W.	1942	,,	Morton, F.
1343	,,	Bullock, W.	1362	,,	Moses, G.
1436	,,	Bushill, F.	1967	,,	Murray, W.
1025	,,	Bushill, H.	2035	,,	Oldfield, E.
1918	,,	Camm, W.	1641	,,	Potts, H.
1783	,,	Clayton, J.	1425	,,	Potts, W.
1943	,,	Cole, R.	2315	,,	Pretty, S.
1917	,,	Cole, W.	1301	,,	Riseley, F.
1645	,,	Cooke, G. W.	1441	,,	Royle, S.
1983	,,	Corry, R.	1484	,,	Smith, J.
2075	,,	Duckworth, E.	1805	,,	Snape, F.
1456	,,	Eastwood, W.	1423	,,	Tovey, C.
1646	,,	Garnett, W.	1389	,,	Wallworth, C. A.
1269	,,	Gibson, L.	1652	,,	Warburton, H.
1984	,,	Goodall, H.	1234	,,	Wardle, T. R.
1491	,,	Hall, H.	1937	,,	Wareing, W.
1604	,,	Harris, A.	2068	,,	Williamson, L.
1438	,,	Haywood, A.	2076	,,	Wright, P.
1797	,,	Higginson, E.	231	,,	Worth, L.

MEN ATTACHED FROM 4TH BATTALION.

1973	L/Corpl.	Davies, S.	1962	Private	Jolliffe, J. W.
1860	Private	Anderson, W.	2049	,,	Kimber, H.
2110	,,	Buckey, J.	1560	,,	Lawler, W.
1942	,,	Byrne, M.	2072	,,	Manley, A.
2101	,,	Cartwright, G.	1916	,,	McMeekin, W.
1388	,,	Cookson, J. G.	1711	,,	Noel, J.
672	,,	Dobson, J. S.	2251	,,	Rhodes, H.
1655	,,	Hall, A.	1886	,,	Ryan, M.
1941	,,	Hewitt, F.	2360	,,	Sweeney, W.
1442	,,	Hughes, G.	2135	,,	Smith, G.

MOBILIZATION AND TRAINING IN ENGLAND.

"B" COMPANY—*Continued.*

DRIVERS (1ST LINE TRANSPORT).

1770	Private	Jones, G.	1715	Private	Rowe, C.
2105	,,	Loftus, P. F.			

COMPANY BATMEN.

2241	Private	Farraday, W. E.	1570	Private	Wightman, P.
2180	,,	Parry, E. A.	2179	,,	Wildig, J. N.
2001	,,	Smith, J.	106	,,	Williams, T.

ATTACHED.

Sergeant Cook		490 Sergeant	Evans, J. C. O.
Transport Sergeant		1250 ,,	Brown, A.
Shoemaker Sergeant		210 ,,	Morris, W.

DRIVERS (1ST LINE TRANSPORT).

1340 Private Ollier, T. (Spare Driver).

PIONEERS.

1566	Private	Jones, J. E.
1459	Private	Chrimes, W. (4th Cheshires).

SIGNALLERS.

858	Sergeant	Pollard, H.	1465	Private	Mills, T. H.
1438	L/Corpl.	Dutton, F. W.	2003	,,	Hogg, W. J.
1379	Private	Bellis, W. T.			

STRETCHER BEARERS.

1187	Private	Acton, A. (7th Cheshires).	2084	Private	Darlington, H.
			2277	,,	Maunder, G.
2243	,,	Cheek, F.			

MEDICAL OFFICER'S ORDERLY.

2249 L/Corpl. Johnson, A.

MACHINE GUNNERS (ATTACHED).

818	Sergeant	Ebrey, W. H.	1431	Private	Green, J.
1263	A/Sergt.	Lockley, T.	1865	,,	Hayles, W. A.
2245	A/Corpl.	Thomas, J. L.	1378	,,	Mitchell, M. O.
1242	L/Corpl.	Johnstone, P.	1571	,,	Pierce, W. A.
1255	,,	Walton, J.	1380	,,	Roberts, T. J.
1240	Private	Ashton, J.	1382	,,	White, G. A.
1873	,,	Baxter, A. J.	1443	,,	Platt, W. W.
1845	,,	Davies, J.			(4th Cheshires).
1459	,,	Formstone, H.			

"B" COMPANY—*Continued.*

MACHINE GUN DRIVERS (1ST LINE TRANSPORT).

2242	Private	Brown, T.	2125	Private	Jones, J. E.
1989	,,	Mathews, J. C.			

MACHINE GUN OFFICER'S BATMAN.

1387 Private Belfield, J.

"C" COMPANY.

Captain C. A. Price
    ,, G. W. C. Hartley
Lieutenant L. G. M. Crick
2nd Lieut. B. S. Walker
    ,, H. F. Davies
    ,, G. McGowan.

5587	A/C.S.M.	Wilcock, J. F.	1592	L/Corpl.	Turner, J. W.
14	C.Q.M.S.	Holland, J.	2138	,,	Walker, F. W.
251	Sergeant	Clare, H.	1698	Drummer	Bottams, S.
70	,,	Evans, F.	1660	,,	Harrop, S.
103	,,	Nicholls, T. G.	1872	,,	Hawkesford, A. H.
62	,,	Sutton, E.	2150	,,	Mills, W.
1553	A/Sergt.	Fisher, P. J.	973	Private	Andrews, D. L.
415	,,	Walker, E.	1590	,,	Andrews, W. S.
1074	,,	Williams, P. H.	1612	,,	Acton, C.
2288	,,	Bishop, F.	1986	,,	Atherton, S. E.
1367	Corporal	Barber, H.	2362	,,	Argyle, L.
1071	,,	Davies, A.	2306	,,	Allman, A. H.
390	,,	Sanders, G.	1303	,,	Beesley, L. C.
422	,,	Sutton, E.	1311	,,	Beesley, W.
398	,,	Sayle, F. C.	1603	,,	Boote, J. H.
1686	A/Corpl.	Oldham, A. E.	1906	,,	Blackburn, S.
2135	,,	Sharpes, G. P.	1929	,,	Bate, T. T.
1600	,,	Lidgett, W.	1864	,,	Barnshaw, F.
607	L/Corpl.	Burton, M.	1301	,,	Bellis, H.
783	,,	Faulkner, G.	1995	,,	Blease, E.
1478	,,	Haddock, A.	2326	,,	Birch, C.
2360	,,	Hughes, J. L.	2307	,,	Bell, T. H.
323	,,	Linley, S.	87	,,	Clarke, W.
1930	,,	Moorefield, C. H.	1650	,,	Calveley, G. H.
1956	,,	Moston, J. H.	1489	,,	Cadman, H.
1971	,,	Rutter, S. B.	1384	,,	Clare, P.
1300	,,	Skillicorn, W.	1496	,,	Clare, J.

"C" Company—*Continued*.

1993	Private	Clarke, P.	1364	Private	Leigh, R.
2363	,,	Coe, F. L.	1494	,,	Leigh, P.
2265	,,	Curzon, L.	2160	,,	Lloyd, R.
2287	,,	Chennery, T. G.	2440	,,	Leary, R.
2312	,,	Chesworth, A.	2311	,,	Lynn, J.
2283	,,	Connors, A. H.	1788	,,	Moulton, T.
2357	,,	Crook, F. C.	295	,,	Millinger, P.
1475	,,	Darlington, J.	1302	,,	Moore, J. G.
1900	,,	Dutton, R.	1904	,,	Miller, A.
2348	,,	Dutton, W. A.	1323	,,	Myatt, R.
1306	,,	Davenport, C.	1927	,,	McHugh, W.
2343	,,	Edwards, H.	2296	,,	Mostyn, J. H.
1473	,,	Fereday, T.	2344	,,	Murphy, W.
1909	,,	Furfie, T.	1987	,,	Norcross, G. H.
2427	,,	Findlow, G.	2133	,,	Nield, F.
1365	,,	Gibbs, S.	2315	,,	Norcott, F.
1386	,,	Gilberts, J.	1474	,,	Oates, J. A.
1767	,,	Gilberts, E.	2158	,,	O'Brien, W.
1773	,,	Green, H.	1907	,,	Palin, T. S.
1926	,,	Guest, J.	2333	,,	Prince, R. N.
1276	,,	Garner, H.	2302	,,	Price, E. M.
1602	,,	Hazlehurst, C.	2314	,,	Price, G. F.
1604	,,	Hignett, G.	2297	,,	Peirce, P. H.
1509	,,	Hughes, T.	2430	,,	Perry, N. H.
1945	,,	Hallsworth, J.	774	,,	Rawlinson, W. A.
1374	,,	Hadden, E.	1797	,,	Radley, T.
2197	,,	Hadden, A.	1905	,,	Roberts, J. F.
2048	,,	Hayes, S.	1045	,,	Rogers, W.
1614	,,	Hayes, W.	1933	,,	Rogers, C. H.
2345	,,	Hedgecock, T.	2289	,,	Riggall, F. S.
2291	,,	Hughes, A. D.	2341	,,	Ravenscroft, P. H.
1655	,,	Hoxworth, T.	2428	,,	Royle, J. W.
1313	,,	Illidge, T. H.	2308	,,	Sumner, W. B.
359	,,	Johnson, J.	2346	,,	Sadler, F.
2149	,,	Jackson, W.	2310	,,	Stolte, W. G.
2077	,,	Jones, J. W.	1772	,,	Thornhill, F.
2351	,,	Jones, J.	1768	,,	Thomason, J.
2361	,,	Jones, W. A.	846	,,	Thornley, G.
2316	,,	Jones, T. P.	1272	,,	Thornley, S.
2300	,,	Jones, W.	950	,,	Turner, E.
2301	,,	Jepson, E. L.	1730	,,	Taylor, J.
2157	,,	Kirkpatrick, T.	2139	,,	Tweedle, G. H.
1998	,,	Kay, H.	1970	,,	Temple, E. J.
1999	,,	Kay, F.	2417	,,	Tilston, W.

"C" COMPANY—*Continued.*

1588	Private	Wilkinson, J.	1359	Private	Watson, J. W.
1340	,,	Worrall, S.	1497	,,	Woodhead, J.
2255	,,	Whitfield, H.	2134	,,	Willis, S. A.
526	,,	Waller, A.	1278	,,	Yould, E. P.
1271	,,	Whitby, R.			

MEN ATTACHED FROM 7TH BATTALION.

1328	L/Corpl.	Gilbert, W. J.	2489	Private	Davies, A.
1776	Private	Astbury, W.	1889	,,	Dunn, O.
1677	,,	Astbury, J. A.	1683	,,	Done, E.
880	,,	Adams, H.	2098	,,	Eaton, A. R.
2174	,,	Ashness, J. W.	1470	,,	Galley, W.
2212	,,	Bradshaw, G.	1507	,,	Hodgkinson, P.
2206	,,	Beard, A.	2373	,,	Hassell, W. J.
1686	,,	Berry, S.	1512	,,	Hatton, W.
1756	,,	Ball, J.	2106	,,	Hordern, H.
1753	,,	Brereton, W.	578	,,	Johnson, R.
2208	,,	Brindley, J. A.	1513	,,	Lightfoot, S.
1206	,,	Broomhall, H.	2544	,,	Phillips, A.
1376	,,	Brown, J.	1661	,,	Pollitt, J.
2091	,,	Clowes, F.	2196	,,	Sadler, J. H.
2300	,,	Cooke, J.	2297	,,	St. Leger, G.
2131	,,	Corbishley, A.	1333	,,	White, C.
1832	,,	Cookson, J. H.	2104	,,	Wilson, P.
1204	,,	Carson, H. E.	1428	,,	Yeardsley, W.

MEN ATTACHED FROM 4TH BATTALION.

1769	Private	Blakeway, J.	1420	Private	Jones J.
2058	,,	Burbie, A.	1704	,,	Latham, G. A.
1605	,,	Blythen, G.	1345	,,	Lewis, R. E.
1856	,,	Bell, H.	1162	,,	Morgan, F.
2127	,,	Cutler, J. E.	1849	,,	Mason, T. C.
1152	,,	Creed, E. A.	2013	,,	Morgan, F.
1670	,,	Cooper, J. G.	2124	,,	Nourse, C. R.
1757	,,	Donovan, J.	1214	,,	Povall, H. B.
1801	,,	Flynn, C.	1215	,,	Roe, S. H.
1852	,,	Hanley, J.	1264	,,	Shone, F.
1489	,,	Hazlehurst, H. S.	1447	,,	Smale, W.
1464	,,	Hickman, C. E.	1502	,,	Walkden, W. C.

DRIVERS (1ST LINE TRANSPORT).

1493	Private	Brazendale, S.	2075	Private	Brazendale, G.
1908	,,	Dale, R. W.			

"C" COMPANY—*Continued*.

COMPANY BATMEN.

1996	Private	Dodson, F.	1308	Private	Pollitt, L.
1063	,,	Lunt, S.	1362	,,	Rigby, H.
1510	,,	Martin, J.	1492	,,	Read, J.

ATTACHED.

Orderley Room Sergeant   452 Sergeant Brown, W.
Sergeant Drummer   1193 Sgt.-Dmr. Walton, H.

DRIVERS (1ST LINE TRANSPORT).

1853	Private	Graham, J. C.	1396	Private	Walker, F.

HEAD QUARTER'S BATMEN.

614	L/Corpl.	Evans, C.	2148	Private	Taylor, G.
2266	,,	Davies, P. G.	1495	,,	Brazendale, J.

PIONEERS.

1315	Private	Done, R.	1280	Private	Vernon, A.

SIGNALLERS.

430	Corporal	Walker, J. W.	783	Private	Hall, W. (7th Cheshires).
1608	Private	Leech, A.			

STRETCHER BEARERS.

2359	Private	Cotgreave, J.	1787	Private	Brooks, H.
1360	,,	Shaw, R.	95	,,	Comley, G.

MACHINE GUNNERS.

1363	L/Corpl.	Moss, F.	2132	Private	Bromley, F.
1653	Private	Boote, T. H.			

MACHINE GUN DRIVERS (1ST LINE TRANSPORT).

315   Private   Leah, J.

"D" COMPANY.

Captain N. B. Ellington
  ,,   A. E. Hodgkin
Lieutenant E. M. Dixon
  ,,   A. H. Cowap
2nd Lieut. C. Johnson
  ,,   H. L. Churton.

"D" COMPANY—*Continued.*

1647	A/C.S.M.	Sweeney, F.	1286	Private	Barlow, F. J.
20	C.Q.M.S.	Darlington, A.	2353	,,	Buckley, J. J.
40	Sergeant	Allen, G.	1676	,,	Bramhall, S.
2137	,,	Gatcliffe, A. C.	1950	,,	Booth, G.
148	,,	Cowley, H.	1822	,,	Cope, A.
1262	,,	Cross, W.	2281	,,	Clarke, S. D.
821	,,	Partin, G.	2285	,,	Chatham, C.
122	,,	Stratford, W. S.	660	,,	Cross, W.
831	A/Sergt.	King, J.	1524	,,	Deakin, J. W.
2189	,,	Crank, C.	2401	,,	Dodd, H.
2188	L/Sergt.	Burns, J.	1526	,,	Dykes, C. P.
2268	,,	Boyle, J. E.	2299	,,	Eason, H.
1436	Corporal	Wilkinson, J. T.	1282	,,	Evans, C. H.
1417	,,	Gerrard, G.	1746	,,	Forster, A.
1638	,,	Billington, S.	1826	,,	Farr, J. W.
1471	,,	Burgess, A.	2089	,,	Griffiths, H.
624	,,	Walton, H.	1680	,,	Gorst, T. L.
1531	A/Corpl.	Bramhall, H.	1955	,,	Hignett, G.
676	,,	Vernon, J. A.	324	,,	Hunter, H.
2280	,,	James, E.	2295	,,	Harrison, A. T.
1472	L/Corpl.	Parkes, J.	2322	,,	Hanley, J.
780	,,	Goodier, F.	2021	,,	Harrop, J.
1672	,,	Rathbone, R.	1952	,,	Hodkinson, J.
2136	,,	Bury, E.	1784	,,	Hand, J.
2259	,,	Pardoe, A.	1515	,,	Harding, G.
2030	,,	Rills, G.	2365	,,	Howells, F. B.
1291	,,	Wilding, H. E.	2085	,,	Hayes, J. W.
1434	,,	Pye, A. E.	1626	,,	Hankey, F.
1136	,,	Day, H.	1825	,,	Houlgrave, J. W.
1325	Drummer	Ball, A.	2367	,,	Jones, T. D.
1183	,,	Leonard, A.	2350	,,	Jones, H.
1780	,,	Wilson, R.	2318	,,	Jones, J.
1760	,,	Gowans, W.	2286	,,	Jones, S.
2337	Private	Atkins, C.	2370	,,	Kemp, J.
2269	,,	Ball, J.	2321	,,	Lloyd, W. A.
1533	,,	Birtwistle, J.	1290	,,	Littlemore, A.
1408	,,	Blount, W. H.	404	,,	Lovatt, C.
1985	,,	Bracegirdle, H.	2319	,,	Langford, W. R.
1690	,,	Buckley, C. W.	2086	,,	Lloyd, T.
2187	,,	Broadhurst, J.	2442	,,	Morley, J.
990	,,	Billington, J.	1260	,,	Manton, F.
716	,,	Baker, J.	2481	,,	Manley, H.
1795	,,	Ball, J.	2186	,,	Mills, P. V.
1681	,,	Butterworth, C.	1522	,,	Mason, A.

"D" Company—*Continued*.

2156	Private	Millington, J.	1794	Private	Vernon, F.
1420	,,	Nichollas, O.	1674	,,	Thorp, P.
1316	,,	Nixon, T. W.	1679	,,	Woodier, J.
1675	,,	Nield, J.	2304	,,	Weeds, G.
1317	,,	Owen, F.	2115	,,	Wright, F.
2061	,,	Owen, W.	2153	,,	Ward, W.
1851	,,	Poole, W. M.	1678	,,	Woodier, J.
844	,,	Perrin, J.	1283	,,	Wood, W.
2355	,,	Prandle. O.	2303	,,	Weeds, E.
1456	,,	Pimblatt, A.	2332	,,	Williams, J. O.
1792	,,	Pine, E. J.	1484	,,	White, L. P.
1799	,,	Perrin, G.	2045	,,	Woods, H.
1521	,,	Postles, H.	1745	,,	Watkins, F.
2091	,,	Parsonage, R.	1485	,,	Wright, J.
2399	,,	Roberts, W. A.	2282	,,	Williams, P.
2155	,,	Robinson, L. H.	1432	,,	Watts, H.
2294	,,	Reynolds, E.	2495	,,	Watts, P.
2088	,,	Rustage, C.	2313	,,	Weeds. J.
2109	,,	Saunders, C.	2284	,,	Watts, L. W.
2349	,,	Spencer, A.	2151	,,	Weedall, A.
2414	,,	Smith, W. H.	852	,,	Williamson, F.
1455	,,	Stubbs, J.	1437	,,	Young, P.
2108	,,	Saunders, J. H.	556	,,	Yates, T.
1733	,,	Shawcross, H.	1637	,,	Yearsley, F.
1644	,,	Trickett, F.			

Men Attached from 7th Battalion.

486	Private	Adkinson, H.	1821	Private	Green, T.
1334	,,	Bate. A. E.	1579	,,	Green. S.
1497	,,	Bailey, J. E.	1729	,,	Gough, A.
1208	,,	Beckett, H.	2030	,,	Gillespie, J. W.
235	,,	Bellfield, J.	2204	,,	Holland, J.
1994	,,	Brandrith, A.	2282	,,	Hoole, J.
1640	,,	Brandrith, G.	793	,,	Holland, G.
1713	,,	Cunningham, S.	1767	,,	Holland, J. C.
2177	,,	Coppack, H.	1212	,,	Hallett, J.
1742	,,	Catterall, A. S.	1332	,,	Howett, R.
1263	,,	Clowes, J.	2178	,,	Harrison, J.
1012	,,	Clarke, J. W.	1998	,,	Ingham, H.
1569	,,	Davenport, G.	1636	,,	Johnson, D.
1385	,,	Davies, G.	1757	,,	Kirkland, R.
1930	,,	Davies, J. W.	1591	,,	Leigh, E.
1248	,,	Floy, J.	1527	,,	Lloyd, F.
2133	,,	Greenwood, C.	2027	,,	McDonald, F. W.

"D" COMPANY—*Continued.*

1999	Private	Mitchell, C.	2050	Private	Ratcliffe, P.
2158	,,	Meredith, F.	1225	,,	Robinson, T.
1905	,,	Mason, H.	1711	,,	Stonley, J.
1834	,,	Mahon, M.	1730	,,	Speed, J.
1993	,,	Mason, G.	1623	,,	Secker, N. F.
1489	,,	Mullins, J.	1597	,,	Thorley, F.
1281	,,	Parker, R.	1338	,,	Ward, R.
1383	,,	Robinson, F.	1279	,,	Wood, S. R.
1633	,,	Roberts, T.	1223	,,	Woolley, J. S.

MEN ATTACHED FROM 4TH BATTALION.

2188	Private	Biddlecomb, R.	2208	Private	Leonard, G.
2184	,,	Connor, T.	2218	,,	Lewis, L. M.
1661	,,	Dewhurst, A.	1575	,,	Middleton, E. R.
1573	,,	Davies, J.	1182	,,	McRae, G.
1430	,,	Eastwood, C.	2042	,,	McEwen, E.
1333	,,	Everett, L.	1364	,,	Mullins, E. S.
2426	,,	Griffiths, T.	1680	,,	Percival, G.
2199	,,	Jones, R.	1681	,,	Rendle, A.
2079	,,	Jones, R.	2019	,,	Thomas, J.
1559	,,	Jellicoe, S.	1361	,,	Wharton, H.
2141	,,	Lindop, A.	1786	,,	Wharton, E.
2189	,,	Leonard, J. P.			

DRIVERS (1ST LINE TRANSPORT).

1682	Private	Coombes, J.	1895	Private	Drinkwater, W.
1793	,,	Wright, F.			

COMPANY BATMEN.

1261	Private	Wright, F.	2293	Private	Blackall, A. W.
1318	,,	Snell, W.	2441	,,	Dodd, H.
2429	,,	Dean, C. A.	1824	,,	Hunter, W.

ATTACHED.

DRIVERS (1ST LINE TRANSPORT).

1550	Private	Bracegirdle, G.

PIONEERS.

1762	Private	Daffern, J.	1504	Private	White, J. W.
1480	,,	Hancock, S.			

SIGNALLERS.

1448	Private	Clarke, J.	1740	Private	Adair, F. C.
1415	,,	Booth, S.	1639	,,	Bloor, J. W.

"D" COMPANY—*Continued.*

STRETCHER BEARERS.

2152	Private	Leech, D.
1642	„	Passey, G.
1161	„	Whitby, J. W. (7th Batt. Ches. Regiment).
1282	„	Warham, T. do.

R. A. M. C. (T.)

725	L/Sergt.	Whittaker, A.	1674	Private	Craze, J. S.
1425	Private	James, J.	1597	„	Williams, A.
1596	„	Hodges, G.			

MACHINE GUNNERS.

1914	Private	Adams, G.	1635	Private	Jones, T.
1738	„	Bostock, S.	1433	„	Southern, J. A.
2184	„	Buckley, W.			

A.S.C. DRIVERS (attached from No. 3 Coy. A.S.C. Welsh Division T.F.)

983	Driver	Strickland, W.	806	Driver	Knowles, A.
846	„	Cowderoy, W.	804	„	Hughes, R.
783	„	Dodd, J.	984	„	Jones, R E.

TRANSPORT ESTABLISHMENT.

Riding Horses	- - -	13	Heavy Draught Horses -	8
Draught „	- - -	26	Pack Animals - - -	9

Total Animals   -   56

Bicycles	- - - -	9	Limbered Wagons - -	3
S.A.A. Cars	- - -	6	Cooks' G.S. Wagon -	1
Maltese Cart	- - -	1	G.S. Wagons - - -	4
Water Carts	- - -	2		

CHAPTER II.

1915.

With the 5th Division.

NEUVE EGLISE : KEMMEL : YPRES : VAUX MARICOURT : BRAY.

THE Battalion left Cambridge, in the early morning of February 14th, in three trains, and proceeded to Southampton, where, on arrival, they were split up into three parts and embarked on the S.S. Oxonian, Manchester Importer and Glenarm Head. The boats left the harbour towards dusk and proceeded to Southampton Water, where a large convoy of transports was assembling. Part of this convoy, with a portion of the Battalion, with its naval escort, crossed the Channel during the night, reaching Le Havre about 9 a.m. The remaining portion of the convoy crossed the following morning and arrived at Le Havre about 1-30 p.m. Each part of the Battalion on arrival, after unloading its stores, proceeded independently to a large rest camp situated on the heights overlooking the town. The weather was bitterly cold, with a strong breeze blowing. The Camp was a canvas one, and as the transport failed to reach camp that evening, a most unpleasant and arctic night was spent, and few will forget their first experience of Active Service campaigning.

The transport negotiated the steep hill to camp the following morning, and the next two days were spent in resting and equipping, all ranks being issued with goatskin jerkins, which caused great amusement to the men, and added a considerable weight to that already carried by them. Orders were received to move on the 17th, and after dinner the Battalion marched to the Station and entrained during the afternoon, in the usual French troop train of cattle trucks. The train left at 6-40 p.m. for an unknown destination, and at 5-30 p.m. the next day came to a halt at Bailleul. On arrival at the station the Battalion was met by a Staff Officer and guides, who directed it to billets in some large greenhouses famed for the cultivation of grapes. Orders were received the next day to join the 14th Brigade of the 5th Division, this Division being in the 2nd Corps (Gen. Sir H. Smith-Dorrien) of the 2nd Army, under General Sir H. Plumer. The Division was under the command of Major-General Morland, and comprised the 13th, 14th, and 15th Infantry Brigades, each Brigade consisting of four Regular and one Territorial Battalion, the 14th Brigade being under the command of Brigadier-General S. Maude, who subsequently became General Sir Stanley Maude. The composition of the Brigades was as follows :—

13TH INFANTRY BRIGADE.

1st Battalion Norfolk Regiment.
1st   „   Bedford Regiment.
1st   „   Cheshire Regiment.
1st   „   Dorset Regiment.
1/6th   „   Cheshire Regiment (T.F.)

14TH INFANTRY BRIGADE.

1st Battalion Devonshire Regiment.
1st   „   East Surrey Regiment.
1st   „   Duke of Cornwall's Light Infantry.
2nd   „   Manchester Regiment.
1/5th   „   (Earl of Chester's) Cheshire Regiment (T.F.)

15TH INFANTRY BRIGADE.

2nd Battalion King's Own Scottish Borderers.
2nd   „   Duke of Wellington's West Riding Regiment.
1st   „   Royal West Kent Regiment.
1st   „   King's Own Yorkshire Light Infantry.
1/9th   „   London Regiment Queen Victoria Rifles (T.F.).

The Battalion left Bailleul about 2-30 p.m. for Neuve Eglise, marching via Dranoutre, where it met some of the 6th Cheshires who were in billets in that neighbourhood. Brigadier-General Maude came out to meet and accompanied the column to the village, which was reached about 5 p.m., after a trying march in pouring rain, billets being taken over from the 1st Devonshire Regiment. The Battalion stayed in this village until March 23rd and received their instruction in trench warfare from the various units of the Brigade.

During this period Bailleul was a very favourite excursion for those off duty, its chief attraction being its shops, which displayed a great quantity of lace, for which the town is famous, and the lunatic asylum, which contained a large number of first-class white enamelled baths, with an ample supply of hot water and towels, which were available for officers and were much used and appreciated by them after a tour in trenches. The Faucon D'or was a very favourite rendezvous, and the opportunity of having a good meal at this hotel under civilized conditions was frequently taken advantage of.

The method of training adopted by the Brigade was progressive and thorough. Company Commanders first of all went up to the trenches with Company Commanders of the Regular Battalions, then Platoon Commanders, Platoons, and finally Companies; at first the men were mixed with those of the regulars in holding the trenches, but subsequently platoons and companies held portions of the sections by themselves, under the command of the units to which they were attached. By this method a thorough instruction in the details of trench work was obtained, as well as the method of carrying out reliefs. The trenches in this section were at the bottom of the Messines Ridge, and were more in the nature of breast works, and in very poor order, and very wet. The approach to them from the Head Quarter Farm, which was Battalion Head Quarters, was along a

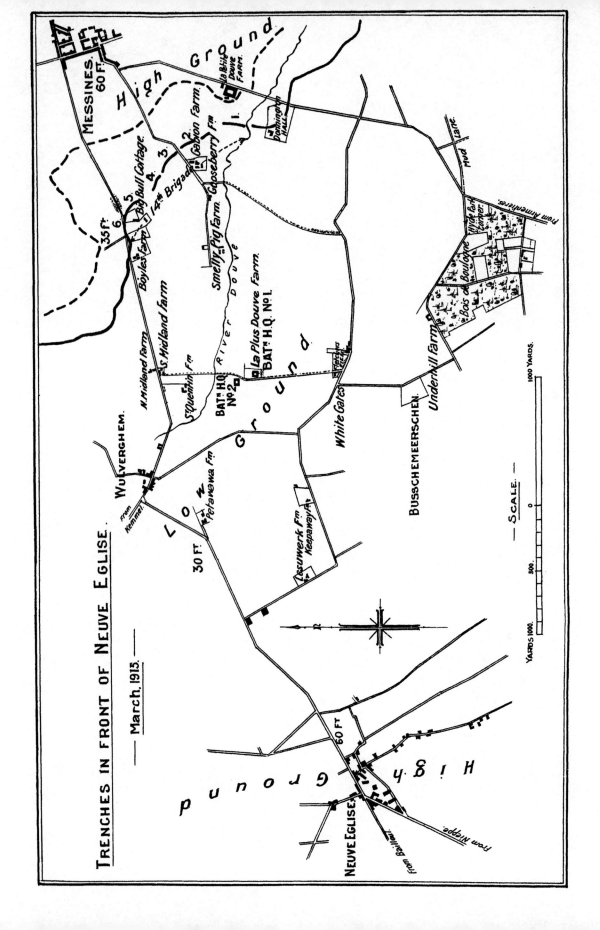

duckboard track and past Smelly Pig and other farms, so called from the number of dead animals lying about the neighbourhood. An alternative but more difficult and muddy route was along the banks of the Douve. The whole area was a waste, and all approach to the trenches had to be made at night, as no communication trenches existed, and the enemy trenches on the ridge commanded a view of all the ground.

It very soon became evident that the village was an unhealthy spot which was shelled regularly, and on February 25th the Battalion had its first casualties, four men being wounded by a shell which landed in the village. Owing to the persistency of the shelling during the day time, orders were received that all troops were to evacuate the village during the day time, and daily excursions were made to out-lying farms, where training was carried on. Whilst here, the Battalion was inspected on March 2nd, in a snowstorm, by the Corps Commander, General Sir H. Smith-Dorrien, the General passing some very complimentary remarks on Territorials and giving all an optimistic impression of the probable duration of the War. During its stay here, various spy hunts took place and, although nothing very tangible resulted, it was pretty certain that a considerable amount of spying was going on in the village amongst the Belgian inhabitants.

On March 23rd the Brigade moved north, and the period of probation and instruction being over, the Battalion took over the Trenches known as J. 1, J. 2, J. 3 L., J. 3 R., H. 4, and J. 10, from the Royal Irish Rifles. Battalion Head Quarters was at Au Rossignol Estaminet, near Kemmel, two Companies being in the line and two in reserve at Locre. The British line in this sector took an almost right-angle turn, so that the road leading to it was subject to a cross fire, and especially in the neighbourhood of the Willows it was no place to dawdle. Another unsavoury spot for the same reason was Support Barn, which sheltered a portion of the supports of the companies in the line.

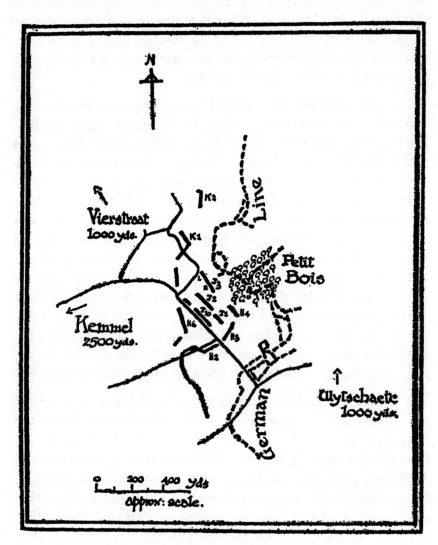

Kemmel Trenches.

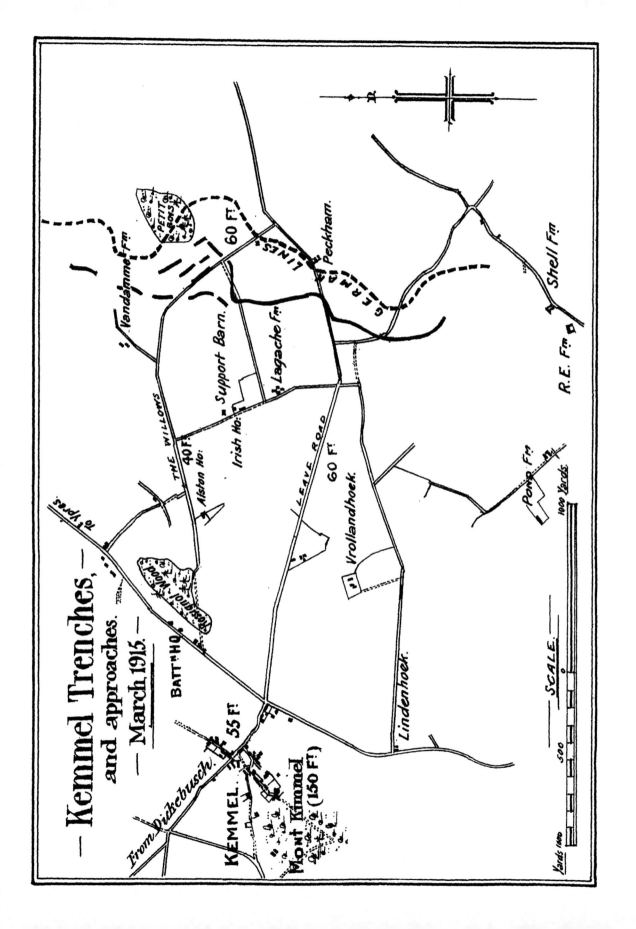

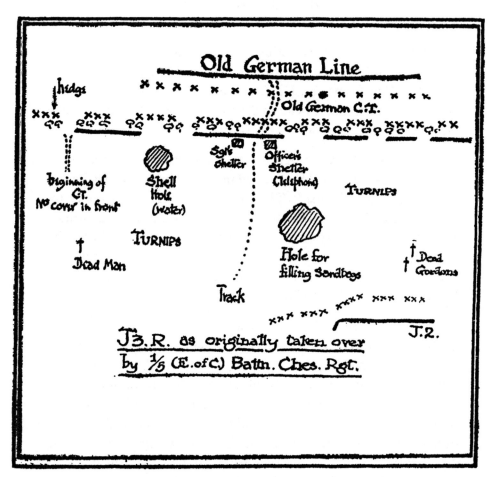

Sketched by Capt. A. E. Hodgkin, M.C.

The trenches themselves were in a deplorable condition, and J. 3 L, and J. 3 R. were especially dangerous, being only 40 yards from the enemy, and with little or no wire in front. The approach to these was over an exposed glacis, which was at night continually being swept with hostile bullets.

The parties approaching these two trenches sustained several casualties, and on one occasion great gallantry was displayed by 2nd Lieut. H. F. Davies and Pte. L. Pollitt in getting in wounded men under heavy rifle fire, Pte. Pollitt being awarded the D.C.M. and Russian Medal of St. George.

On Easter Monday, April 5th, the Battalion was relieved by the 2nd Battalion Royal Scots, and moved to huts near Dickebush, and on the 7th to Ypres. The same night " A " Company took over No. 27 Trench from the 1st Battalion Cheshire Regiment, with " B " Company in support at Spoilbank, Battalion Head Quarters taking over those of the same Battalion at Spoilbank, " C " and " D " Companies being in reserve, with the Quarter Master's stores, at the Cavalry Barracks, Ypres.

The route from Ypres to the trenches ran along a dreary stretch of road to Chateau Lankhof, which had a great reputation for " overs," and thence along the Canal Bank to Spoilbank, which was a cutting through which the Ypres-Commines Canal ran, with high and well-wooded banks on either side. Here was accommodation for Battalion Head Quarters and one Company in support, in rather uncomfortable shelters excavated in the bank, the Battalion Dressing Station being at Chester Farm, on the opposite side of the Canal. The trenches were about three-quarters of a mile in front. No. 27 when first taken over was more of the nature of a sandbag breast work, with little trench or parados, the distance to the German trenches varying from 60 to 100 yards. The German trenches were on the crest of the hill, and ours on the up slope, and it was evident that they had been

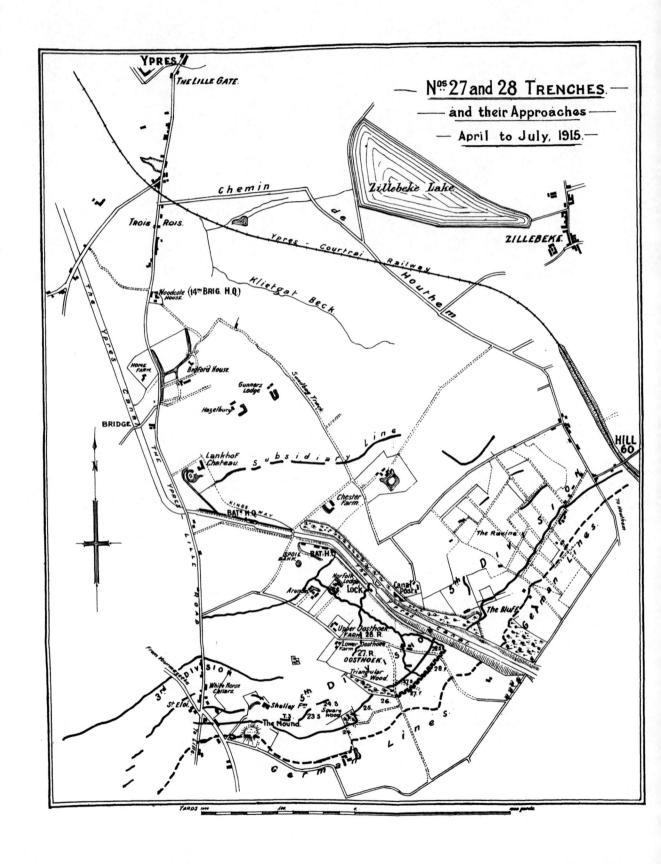

gradually constructed where a battle had ended. There were a number of dead men buried very lightly in the trenches, which made any improvements in many parts almost impossible. There were practically no shelters, and those that did exist merely gave cover from weather and not from fire. Reliefs were worked by two companies going into the line and two companies resting at Ypres in reserve. On April 17th a great mine was exploded by the British, followed by an attack on Hill 60, a little to the north, the Companies in the line assisting in the scheme of attack by vigorous supporting fire on the enemy trenches in front.

At this period Ypres was being heavily shelled day and night with high explosive and incendiary shells, and the Cavalry Barracks had to be evacuated. The Companies at Ypres moved to bivouacs near the Canal, and set up trench bivouac sheets, but in consequence of the shelling spreading, these also had to be evacuated, and a move was made to a Factory on the outskirts of the town, and later further out still to bivouacs at Kruisstraat.

On April 22nd the Germans, with the aid of Gas, made a partial break through North of the town, and the two Companies at rest were ordered to proceed with two days' rations to the reserve line of trenches. Arrangements were made for a possible retirement of the troops holding the line, in case of the salient having to be abandoned, but owing to the great stand made by the Canadians and British troops on the north holding the enemy up, this eventuality did not materialize. As the enemy pressure had slackened, the line was now held rather more thinly, and on May 8th Trench No. 28 was taken over by the Battalion, in addition to No. 27. This new trench was on the S.E. side of the Commines Canal, and ran from the Canal towards 27, but was not connected with it, there being a gap of 200 yards between the two trenches, with a marsh in the centre. The trenches were subsequently joined up by the Battalion during the following two months. All four companies were now in the line, and continued there until May 12th, when they went out for a much required rest to Dickebush to bivouac under bivouac sheets. As this form of cover was not healthy for the men, owing to the continuous wet, a large number of them developed temperatures, and as they were shewing signs of wear and tear, owing to their work in the line, and the manifold fatigues up to the line as carrying and working parties when at rest, the Battalion moved to billets at Boeschepe on May 24th, where it rested for a week. Here they first saw some of Kitchener's first hundred thousand about whom so much had been heard, and whose arrival acted as a tonic, and greatly raised the spirits of the men. On June 1st the Battalion again moved up and took over numbers 27 and 28 from the 1st Battalion Devonshire Regiment.

On June 17th a move was made back to Dickebush for a fortnight's rest until July 1st, when a weekly system of reliefs came into operation. During the rest at Dickebush, Brigadier-General Maude inspected the Battalion and bade them good-bye on his leaving the Brigade to take up another command, the command of the Brigade being taken over by Brigadier-General Compton.

At the beginning of July, during the Battalion's tour in the trenches, some platoons of the 7th Battalion King's Royal Rifles (Kitchener's) were attached to the Battalion for instruction in trench warfare, and on July 14th parties of the 6th Duke of Cornwall's Light Infantry were attached for a similar purpose.

On July 16th a cricket match was played against the 14th Field Ambulance, on the best pitch that could be selected. The Battalion XI. went in first and scored over 100 for 8 wickets, when rain stopped play. Several batsmen shewed first class form on a dangerous wicket, and the casualties were nil.

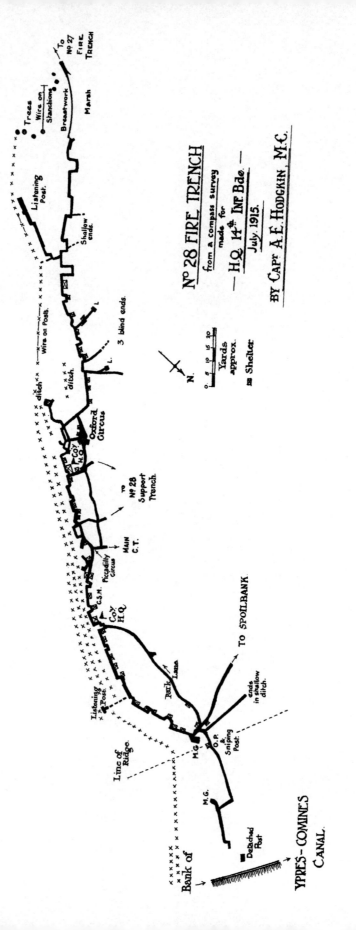

At the end of July it was announced that the 5th Division was to be relieved and taken out of the line, to form a nucleus of a new army that was being formed, owing to the arrival of strong reinforcements, and on July 24th the Battalion was relieved by the 2nd Battalion Suffolk Regiment, and moved to Reninghelst, and subsequently to Eeke, where they went into billets on July 26th. The following day the 14th Brigade paraded and were reviewed by the 2nd Army Commander, General Sir H. Plumer, who, in the course of his remarks when addressing the troops, said that he had not come there that morning to hold an inspection parade, but rather to say a few words to the Brigade before it left to join the new Army to which it was being transferred.

He was glad to say that the long period during which the men had been engaged in trench warfare had not caused them to forget how to stand still and to handle their arms; their clothing was against them and it would not have pleased those who were used to Aldershot parades, but those who really knew soldiers were able to judge, in spite of the clothing, and the Brigade had turned out as it ought to have done.

The General went on to say that he need not remind his hearers of what they had done in the past, for that would be found written in the records which would form the History of the War. Those, however, who were acquainted with the facts knew the part which the 5th Division and the 14th Infantry Brigade had taken in the early part of the War, and they knew that that part had been at least an arduous one.

During the period that the Brigade had been in the sector which it was then leaving, it had been occupied with trench warfare rather than with active operations against the enemy, with one or two exceptions when, although not actually employed as a Brigade, two of its Battalions—the Devons and the East Surreys—had been very hotly engaged at " Hill 60," and by their efforts had contributed very greatly to the retention of that Hill.

Since that time the Brigade had continued to be engaged in trench warfare, but trench warfare had not to be rated the dull sort of fighting that some were prone to think, as Army Commanders knew full well. Comparisons, the General remarked, were odious, but he had no hesitation in saying that, so far as the 2nd Army was concerned, and, for that matter, so far as the Expeditionary Force was concerned, no Brigade had won so high a reputation for trench warfare as had the 14th Brigade under General Maude.

During the operations that had taken place in the Ypres salient, the 14th Brigade had been engaged in fighting which might be characterised as " dull " from the newspaper point of view, but the General reminded his hearers that, unless a commander can rely on the troops that are holding the line, he cannot withdraw troops as he otherwise might for fighting elsewhere. Whilst commanding the 5th Corps he knew that the line occupied by the Brigade was absolutely safe, and, he added, it was to the Officers, Non-commissioned Officers and men whom he was addressing that he ascribed as much credit as he did to those who were engaged in the more active fighting.

The Army Commander concluded by saying that the Brigade was going to a new Army under General Munro, and to a new Corps under General Morland respectively, both of whom knew full well the reputation of the Brigade. On those whom he was addressing would devolve the responsibility of living up to the reputation which they had made and of forming the nucleus of the new Army, for they would be the veterans, and the 14th Brigade standard would be the standard which other Brigades would emulate; it must and would be a high one, and if all the other Brigades reached it, both the Army and the Corps Commander would have confidence. The General then expressed sorrow that the Brigade was parting from the 2nd Corps and the 2nd Army, and wished them the best of luck.

During their stay in the Ypres Sector the Battalion had had a very hard time, the weather, especially in the early part of the year, being very bad and cold. Their periods of so-called rest when not in the line were only periods of absence of strain from actually holding the trenches, as large working parties and parties for carrying engineering and other stores had to be furnished nightly, involving heavy and trying marches, which resulted in the men composing these rarely getting back much before dawn, and on one occasion, after an exceptionally severe period of fatigues of this nature, the order for a tour of duty in the trenches was received by the men with loud cheers.

A great amount of work had been put in in improving the trenches. No. 27 had been joined to No. 28 across the marsh by means of building sandbag parapets on a foundation of corrugated iron sheets, a new support trench had been constructed in rear of Nos. 27 and 28, and a communication trench had been dug from the canal cutting which served both Nos. 27 and 28. Shelters had also been erected in the trenches, which were not only more comfortable for the men but more secure against fire. The Battalion Head Quarters at Spoilbank had been greatly enlarged and improved, new shelters having been constructed for the men and a new regimental aid post having been built and made shrapnel proof.

The casualties of the Battalion up to this date were caused chiefly by sniping (a form of warfare in which the Germans at this stage showed a great superiority) and by shell fire. 2nd Lieutenants B. S. Walker, H. F. Davies and Drummond Fraser, and 39 N.C.O's. and men were killed, Captain A. E. Hodgkin and Captain W. Rogers, R.A.M.C., Lieutenant E. M. Dixon, 2nd

Lieutenants C. Johnson, A. H. Jolliffe, C. N. Holmstrom, G. Gledhill, and 223 N.C.O's. and men were wounded. A considerable number of Officers and men had gone to Hospital sick, and although some reinforcements had been sent up, the strength of the Battalion had dropped to under 750.

After resting at Eeke until August 1st the Battalion marched to Godewaersvelde Station, and there entrained, reaching Corbie, on the Somme, the following morning, where they were billeted for one night, moving the next day to Daours. Being the first British troops in this part since September, 1914, the Battalion had a great reception from the French inhabitants. Here the Battalion, with the rest of the 14th Brigade, was inspected by the new Army Commander, General Sir Charles Munro, K.C.B., and the same night marched to Treux and Ville sur Ancre. The new Army was taking over a part of the line from the French, and the Sector allotted to the Brigade was the right Sector, resting on the river Somme at Eclusier, the French continuing the line to the south of that Village.

The Sector allotted to the Cheshires was that on the extreme right. To carry out the relief the Battalion moved on August 8th to Suzanne, an advance party having gone on to make a reconnaisance of the Sector, and the following day took over from the French 24th Regiment. The relief was carried out without a hitch, and many pleasant reminiscences remain of the hospitality and *bonhomie* of our French Allies.

The Sector held by the Battalion was a great change from that in the Ypres area. The Somme at this point made a large loop in the shape of an inverted '∩' with high banks on each outer side. The west side of the loop was held by the English, and the east side by the enemy; the ground between was intersected with streamlets and was marshy and thick with trees and undergrowth. This was " No Mans Land." On taking over, "A" Company

Vaux sur Somme.

went to Dragon's Wood, " B " Company to Vaux Wood, " C " Company to Vaux, with Head Quarters and " D " Company at Suzanne. The work here was mainly that of outposts and patrols. A causeway ran out into the marsh from Vaux for about 200 yards, and a small post, called Duck Post, was established at the end of it. This was a most important post, as it commanded the only means of access across the marsh and was the exit point for all patrols. Patrolling was done by boat as well as by land. The Battalion Scouts were in charge of Lieutenant F. Bishop, who did some very fine work here. A party of Indian Scouts (Pathans) were also attached to the Battalion, under Captain Jones. The enemy adopted the same tactics, and several encounters took place between opposing patrols. It was during one of these encounters, close to Duck Post, that 2nd Lieutenant F. T. Vernon was killed, a German prisoner being captured on the same occasion.

This Sector on our arrival was very quiet, but soon livened up, as our artillery became rather aggressive, the Chapeau Gendarme and " Y " Wood being very favourite targets.

A very fine Observation Post existed in Vaux Wood, from which the whole of the enemy's trench system could be overlooked, and the Battalion also had a post in this Wood from which observation was kept daily, some very valuable intelligence information being obtained of the enemy's movements. The two villages on either side of the loop, Vaux on our side and Curlu on the enemy's, were not shelled at all, presumably to avoid retaliation on either side, both being occupied by troops. Vaux was also occupied by civilians at this time.

The 6th Liverpools had by this time joined the Brigade, making it a six Battalion Brigade, and on September 2nd the Battalion was relieved by them and returned to Suzanne for a week, returning to their old Sector again on the 9th and remaining until the 21st, on which date they moved north and took over trenches 28, 29, 30, 31, 32, 33, 34, and 35 from the 1st Battalion Devonshire Regiment, with Head Quarters at Maricourt. The front taken over was a very extended one and necessitated three Companies being in the line, with one in support, " A " Company being on the right, Nos. 34 and 35; " B " in the centre, Nos. 31, 32, and 33; and " D " on the left, Nos. 28, 29 and 30; with " C " in support. The trenches in this Sector were deep, but required a great amount of repair, and as they were not continuous but of the " T " type, communications were very long. In addition there were some advanced posts at the heads of saps which were continually a source of considerable anxiety. Instruction in trench warfare was here given to the 11th Worcesters, who had recently come out from England.

Owing to the extended front held by the Brigade, reliefs were very difficult, and the Battalion here held the line for the extremely long period of 33 days without any relief (except that " C " Company relieved " B " in the centre sector) until October 26th, when on relief by the Duke of Cornwall's Light Infantry they took over the Maricourt Village defences from the 2nd Manchesters.

Whilst in Maricourt considerable improvements were carried out on the defences of the village. On November 13th the Battalion, on relief by the East Surreys, again took over the Vaux Sector, Head Quarters moving into Vaux Village, which had by this time been evacuated by the civilians.

The following is an extract from the 14th Brigade Summary of November 15th, 1915 :—" 5th Cheshire Regiment have done excellent work in Maricourt."

On November 29th the Battalion was relieved by the 9th Royal Scots, and moved back to Bray (where billets were secured by the river) for the purpose of taking

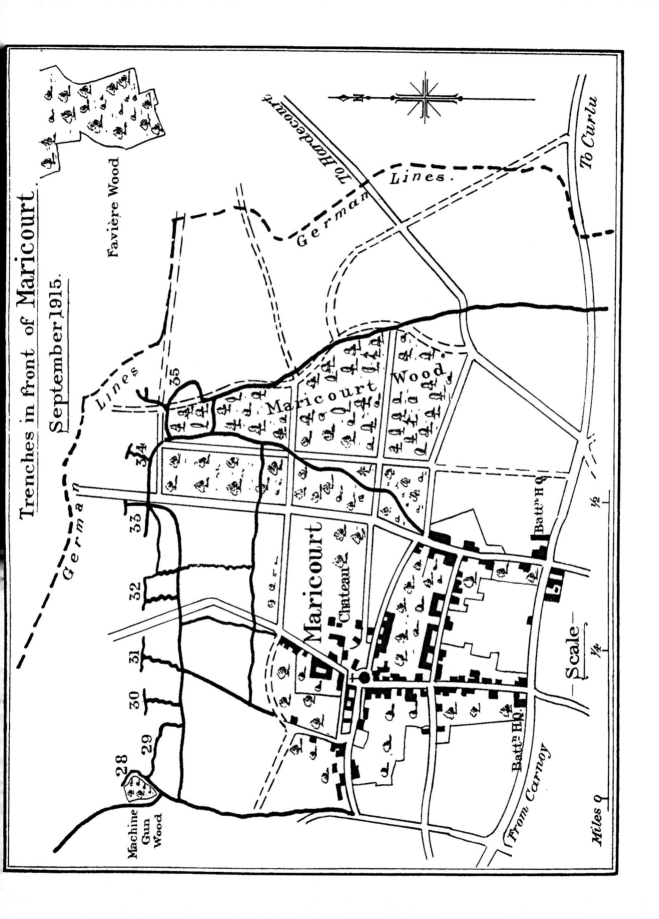

up the duties of Pioneer Battalion to the Division, the Battalion having been specially selected for this onerous duty on account of the high reputation it had earned for itself in trench construction and pick and spade work. After having been officially appointed and been ordered to prepare indents for the full equipment of tools for a " Pioneer Battalion," this order was cancelled on the grounds that " Territorial Battalions were not to be appointed as Pioneers to Regular Divisions. The 1/5th Cheshires were, however, to carry on with these duties until further orders." This order was again changed later in 1916.

At the end of the year, owing to the arrival of strong reinforcements from home, several new divisions were in course of formation, and to meet these changes the Brigade, which had become rather unweildy owing to the additional Battalions attached to it, was reorganized, being reduced to four Battalions. A large number of Territorial Battalions had been attached to Regular Brigades, and most of these were taken away and formed into fresh Territorial Divisions. In addition, each Division was to have a Pioneer Battalion, quite a new formation for the British Army. Several of these had undergone training as such in England, but there were not enough of them to provide the numbers required, and the additional ones needed were to be formed from the surplus Territorial Battalions. During this period of re-organization the Battalion at Bray, employed as a Pioneer Battalion, was engaged in the construction of a series of cut and cover shelters for itself, which it was ordered to construct owing to the congestion of billets in Bray, and also in making mined Divisional Battle Head Quarters. The construction of these works brought into prominence the capability of the Battalion for skill in constructional work, and by February 1st the dug-outs were completed and occupied by the Battalion. These new quarters were of a very elaborate type, complete with bunks for every man, kitchens and store quarters, together with an Officers'

Mess and sleeping accommodation for a full establishment of Officers. They were completely shrapnel proof, and were probably the finest of their type on the British Front. They were named The Barracks, Earl of Chester Street, and at a later date were called Groves Town, after the Colonel's name. Work was also carried on in Lucknow, Peronne, and Suffolk Avenues, and on Wellington and Lucknow redoubts, and during operations in connection with these 2nd Lieutenant W. E. Davies was killed through shell fire. A new fire trench was also constructed on the old front at Maricourt by " D " Company, in front of No. 31 trench, this Company moving to Suzanne for the purpose. On January 25th orders were received that the 5th Cheshires had been appointed Pioneer Battalion to the 56th (London) Division, in course of formation, and to be commanded by General Sir Amyatt Hull, K.C.B. On leaving the 14th Brigade the following order was issued by the Brigadier:—" In saying farewell to the 5th Battalion Cheshire Regiment, which is leaving the 14th Brigade and being formed into a Pioneer Battalion, the Brigadier places on record his very high appreciation of the excellent work of the Battalion since it joined the Brigade. The conduct of the 5th Cheshires both in the field and in billets has been exemplary, and the fact that they have been selected for formation into a Pioneer Battalion is proof of the excellence of their work. The Brigadier-General thanks all ranks for the loyal services they have at all times given, and wishes the Battalion the best of luck in the future."

The following Battalion order was also issued:—

To all Officers, Warrant Officers, N.C.O's and men of the
1/5th (Earl of Chester's) Battalion, the Cheshire Regiment.

As Commanding Officer I desire to promulgate to all ranks of the Battalion the following personal letters received by me.

The first is from Brig. Gen. C. W. Compton, C.M.G., on the Battalion leaving the 14th Infantry Brigade, and the second is from Major Gen. C. T. Mc. M. Kavanagh, C.V.O., C.B., D.S.O., on the Battalion leaving the 5th Division, to take up its appointment as Pioneer Battalion to the 56th Division.

(1) "My Dear Groves,

I regret very much that it will not be possible for me to see your fine Battalion on parade before you leave the 14th Brigade, as I should have liked to tell your men how highly I value the excellent work they have done since I had the honour of taking over the Brigade.

I am publishing a farewell order and I hope you will understand that this is no formal order but is only a slight tribute to your Battalion for all we owe to them.

To you personally I am deeply indebted for the great assistance you have always so readily given me, and I am truly sorry that it has been found necessary in the interests of the service, to take you out of my Command.

I shall always have a very happy recollection of our association together.

I hope to see most of your Officers before they go, but in case I should not do so will you please tell them that I thank them all most heartily for their good work and wish them all the best of luck in anything they may be called upon to do while the War lasts.

      Yours sincerely,
28/11/15.   (Signed) C. W. COMPTON."

(2) "My Dear Colonel,

Before your Battalion leaves the 5th Division, I am writing to tell you how very sorry both I and the whole Division are at their departure. They have done really good work both in the trenches and when employed as a Pioneer Battalion, since I have been in command of the Division, and I have been much struck by the good and cheerful spirit shown by all ranks however unpleasant the work was they were asked to do.

The whole Division, I know, will join with me in wishing you and the Battalion the best of luck in the future, and we shall all watch its career with the greatest interest, and will feel that the good work it is sure to do in the future will add to the credit of the 5th Division.

      Yours sincerely,
    (Signed) C. M. KAVANAGH, Major Gen.,
      Commanding 5th Division."

I also desire to take this opportunity of expressing to all ranks my deep and sincere gratitude for the manner in which they have always supported me in carrying out the tasks, sometimes difficult ones, which the Unit has been called upon to perform.

The Honour recently conferred upon your Commanding Officer by His Most Gracious Majesty the King, must be taken by all ranks as a distinct appreciation by higher Command of the efforts of all to do their duty to their King and Country in this long and tedious war.

(Signed) JOHN E. G. GROVES, Lt. Colonel,
Commanding 1/5th Batt. Cheshire Regiment.

31st January, 1916.

The last paragraph in the order refers to Lieut.-Colonel Groves having been appointed a Companion of the Order of St. Michael and St. George by His Majesty the King.

On February the 2nd the Battalion left " The Barracks " and marched to Corbie, and thence, *via* St. Gratien and Domart, to Hallencourt, where it joined the new 56th Division, being almost the first troops to arrive.

The doings of the Battalion from its arrival in France to this date were chronicled in the following lines composed by the late 2297 Sergeant P. H. Peirce :—

1/5th (E. of C.) BATTALION.

A Rhyming Account of the Battalion since their Landing in France.

WHEN Wilhelm's head had swelled (alas!) to disproportionate size,
He thought to boss the Universe with England for a prize:
So, scorning sacred treaties and a monarch's plighted word,
He sent his armies far and wide and bade them use the sword.
But other Powers decreed that he the penalty should pay,
For trusting in brute strength and force to win the toasted " Day,"
And England with her ancient sense of what is wrong and right.
Called on her sons to prove her cause, and go forth to the fight.

Right loyally did Cheshires rise their privilege to claim,
Inspired by earlier records and their deeds of deathless fame;
And not the least the 5th Battalion—Earl of Chester's own—
Left England's shores and landed safely in Le Havre town.
Two nights we stayed, one cold, one wet, and then we marched away,
And boarded trucks—like cattle packed—to take us to the fray.
For two score hours we bumped along, and rocked and rolled and clattered,
And criticised the Government and other things that mattered.

Then at Bailleul we heard the guns but slept the none less soundly,
Arising stiff but feeling fit to trounce the Huns right roundly.
And later on in face of snow, and rain, and hail, and sleet,
Reached Neuve Eglise right glad at last to ease our aching feet.

At Neuve Eglise experience gained in shot and shell and trenches,
With extras (gratis) in the shape of aeroplanes and stenches:
And midnight marches—weary miles of pitfalls, mud and holes
Increased in us the right to doubt the safety our *soles*.
From Neuve Eglise to Kemmel—two days rations in our packs,
(We nearly fainted when presented with some coke in sacks:)
But dodging sundry bullets found at length a "home from home,"
And fell asleep a wondering why the deuce we'd ever come.
From thence to Ypres we marched one night, right glad to see a City,
Despite the havoc wrought by Huns, and voted it a pity,
That "Allemands," like Goths of old, should wreck historic places,
While posing as the rightful leaders of the cultured races.

The weather growing hotter we at last began to stew,
Tormented by the flies and other forms of "Hitchy-koo";
And interesting groups were seen all seated on the ground,
Comparing notes and specimens of "mighty atoms" found.

At length we said good-bye to Ypres and thence by road and rail,
We came to Vaux which adds another chapter to our tale;
For here disdaining trenches we went forth to meet the foe,
And on more than one occasion played a game of touch and go.
'Twas a peaceful little village, but the neighbours o'er the way
Insisted on their dubious right in our backyard to play:
Each time they came with "fireworks" armed, although they knew 'twas wrong.
But strange to say their visits never lasted very long.
Thence to Suzanne and Maricourt, in trenches once again,
Accompanied in the usual way by drenching showers of rain;
And having formerly endured a perfect plague of gnats,
Extended our acquaintance to amazing hosts of rats!

The longest yarn will have an end as does the longest "street,"
But ere I close this chronicle, I think 'tis only meet
To mention that with spade and pick we gained a lasting fame,
And earned our right as Englishmen to say we played the game.
So from the firing line we marched and shortly came to Bray,
(Expressive word which warns me that I'd better close this Lay);
For War or Peace 'tis work that tells whene'er there's work to do,
And having said my say I'll add one final word—"Adieu."   P. H. P.

CHAPTER III.

1916.

With the 56th Division.

GOMMECOURT : SOMME : LAVENTIE.

THE 56th (London T.F.) Division was composed of first line Territorial units, recruited from the City and County of London and Middlesex.

The constitution of the Division was as follows :—

Divisional Commander	Major Gen. Sir C. P. A. Hull, G.C.B.
G. S. O., 1	Lt. Col. J. Brind, D.S.O.
A. A. and Q. M. G.	Lt. Col. Grubb, D.S.O.
C. R. E.	Lt. Col. H. W. Gordon, D.S.O.

INFANTRY BRIGADES.

167TH BRIGADE (Brig. Gen. Nugent).

1/1st Battalion London Royal Fusiliers.
1/3rd   „   „   „   „
1/7th   „   Middlesex Regiment.
1/8th   „   „   „

168TH BRIGADE (Brig. Gen. G. G. Loch, C.M.G., D.S.O.)

1/4th Battalion London Royal Fusiliers.
1/12th   „   London Regiment (Rangers).
1/13th   „   „   „   (Kensingtons).
1/14th   „   „   „   (London Scottish).

169TH BRIGADE (Brig. Gen. E. S. D'E. Coke, C.M.G., D.S.O.)

1/2nd Battalion London Royal Fusiliers.
1/5th   „   London Regiment (London Rifle Brigade).
1/9th   „   „   „   (Queen Victoria Rifles).
1/16th   „   „   „   (Queen's Westminsters).

ENGINEERS—416th Field Company (Edinburgh).
         512th   „   „   (London).
         513th   „   „   (London).
PIONEER BATTALION—1/5th Batt. (E. of C.) Cheshire Regiment.
ARTILLERY (Brig. Gen. R. J. G. Elkington, C.M.G., D.S.O.)
   280th, 281st and 282nd Brigades R.F.A. (London).
R. A. M. C.—2/1st London Field Ambulance.
        2/2nd   „   „   „
        2/3rd   „   „   „
H. Q. and 4 Companies A.S.C. and Detachment of R.A.V.C.

As a Pioneer Battalion was a new formation, it will be convenient to explain what its establishment was and what duties it had to perform.

A Pioneer Battalion is " Infantry " and " Divisional Troops." It is composed of Head Quarters, and four Companies divided into platoons and subdivided into sections (this was subsequently altered to three companies but with no reduction in numbers). It is armed exactly the same as an Infantry Battalion and has the same specialists—Signallers, Bombers, Lewis Gunners, etc. Its transport is considerably larger than that of an Infantry Battalion, as each Company has two G.S. Wagons for tools. Its training consists of two parts :—(I.) Infantry; (II.) Pioneer. This is owing to the dual rôle it has to play, namely, that it must be trained and capable of taking the part of Infantry of the Line if occasion demands it, as well as being capable of carrying out engineering duties, either by itself or in conjunction with Royal Engineer Companies. Its chief work is that of Field Engineering, and it is only in emergency that it is called upon to act as Infantry. The work carried out is almost entirely battle zone work, and its great object in all offensives is to help towards the successful exploitation of an attack, which largely depends upon the speed and skill with which communications (roads, bridges, tracks and tramways) are repaired or constructed. The movements of reserves, the advance of artillery, the supply of ammunition for the guns, the getting forward of supplies of food, water and ammunition to the infantry, as well as reliefs and the evacuation of the wounded are largely dependent upon the rapidity with which communications are restored and new tracks and routes constructed. Its object is not to " make " roads or communications in the ordinary sense of the word, but rather to make such means of progress temporarily passable as quickly as possible, leaving the subsequent permanent improvement to troops in rear. One of the most important duties in this connection is that of road reconnaissance, which demands speed and accuracy, and is vital to the successful organization of engineering operations, this being one of the tasks which was frequently allotted to Pioneer Officers.

The duties of a Pioneer Battalion during trench warfare (chiefly trench construction, repair and wiring) were very arduous, as, being in the battle zone, they had to be carried out in nearly every case at night owing to enemy observation, and involved long and trying marches up to the site of work and back, frequently under shell fire, as the approach areas were always the subject of the enemy's artillery attention in the evenings. These demanded a high standard of training and skill on the part of Officers and non-commissioned officers in finding their way to, and setting out the work, a by no means easy task in pitch darkness, when the site is only described by a map reference.

On February 27th the Battalion left Hallencourt and had a very trying march owing to the depth of snow on the roads to Domart, where it stayed for fourteen days and received its Pioneer outfit of tools. On March 12th it moved to Authieule, near Doullens, and on the 15th to Grand Rullecourt. The whole of this village was allotted to the Battalion, and Lieut.-Colonel J. E. G. Groves was appointed Commandant of the Area.

Good billets were obtained, and the village, which was in a very dirty state, was given a thorough spring cleaning. Horse lines were built, incinerators erected, and innumerable sanitary improvements were carried out. The new establishment of tools and transport had arrived and re-organization was carried out. This entailed a sorting out of the men, so that each Company should have its quota of skilled tradesmen. The method adopted was to create in each Company one platoon composed of skilled men, which was called a " specialist " platoon, and into these were drafted all the bricklayers, joiners, carpenters, plumbers, and other tradesmen. The scheme proved satisfactory and enabled each Company to act independently should occasion arise, but on the other hand it had its disadvantages, as was shown on one or two occasions when a large shell falling in the middle of one of these platoons caused many casualties amongst tradesmen whom, more especially towards the end of the war, it was impossible to replace. A Sapper Section was also raised, composed of handy men, which was attached to Head Quarters and was of the utmost value, as the men were chiefly selected for their experience in mining and tunnelling work.

The various units to compose the Division were gradually arriving in the area, and by the beginning of May the 56th Division was complete and ready for action.

In the first week in May the Hebuterne Sector of the front was taken over by the Division, which now became part of the VII. Corps of the 3rd Army. The 5th Cheshires moved to Souastre on May 6th, " B " Company marching to Hebuterne and occupying " The Keep " to act as reserve to the 167th Brigade in the line, " C " Company moving to Halloy on the 9th to work under 169th Brigade. " A " Company, which had been temporarily detached to Givenchy le Noble, joined the Battalion later. During the months of May and June a great amount of work was done on the roads in the district, which were in a bad condition, in preparation for an offensive, quarries being opened and worked to obtain the necessary material. New dry weather tracks were laid out and dumps and dug-outs constructed. This work was done by two Companies, the other two doing trench repair and reconstruction in the line, which was in a poor condition.

Whilst in this village the Battalion received orders to transform a barn into a theatre for the Divisional Concert Party, which had recently been formed. This was accomplished without any difficulty, a stage being erected by the Battalion carpenters and seating accommodation provided by the utilisation of the chesses from Royal Engineer pontoon wagons. The troupe, which was called " Bow Bells," gave their first performance on May 15th, the success of which foretold great possibilities for the future, which were subsequently more than realised. The original entertainment given was a pierrot performance, but later short revues, musical comedies, and an annual pantomime were produced.

At the end of the month an entirely new front line was dug, about 400 yards in advance of the old line, by a whole Brigade in two nights, May 26th—27th and 27th—28th. The duty of the Cheshires was to connect this trench with the old one by means of a communication trench, a composite company under Captain Bairstow carrying this work out. During June it became evident that active operations were pending, as two 15-inch howitzers arrived at Souastre and took up positions just outside the village, and " A " and " C " Companies left to practise their duties in an attack with 168 and 169 Brigades. Orders finally came through for the operations.

The objective of the 56th Division was to capture and consolidate a line running approximately due North from Strong Point K. 11. c. to junction of Fillet and Indus, joining hands with the 46th Division who were to continue the line from this point to the " little Z," and then clear Gommecourt Village and

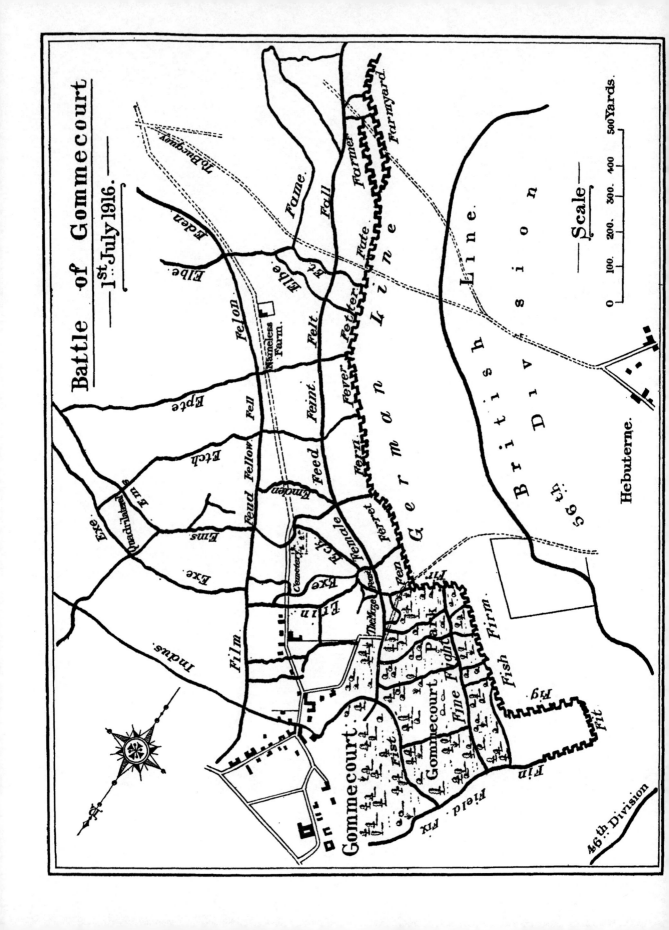

Park. The Division was ordered to attack on a front of two Brigades, which were given the following objectives :—

168th Infantry Brigade on the right, attacking on a front of two Battalions was to capture the Strong Point at K. 11. c., Fame, Elbe, between Fame and Felon, Felon, junction of Felon and Epte. Strong Points to be consolidated at K. 11. c., Elbe and Et. S.E. of Nameless Farm, junction of Felon and Epte.

169th Infantry Brigade on the left, attacking on a front of two Battalions was to capture Fell, Fellow, Feud, Cemetery, The Maze, Fir and junction of Fir and Firm. A third Battalion was to push through up Ems and Etch, capture and consolidate Quadrilateral in K. 5. a., bomb up Fillet, and establish a post to join 46th Division at junction of Fillet and Indus. Strong Points to be established at junction of Fir—Firm, The Maze, Cemetery.

The attack was to be preceded by a bombardment lasting from 24th to 30th June, during which there were to be two discharges of smoke.

The following duties were assigned to the Battalion :— " C " Company (Capt. E. M. Dixon), attached to 168 Brigade, was to wire three strong points in the enemy's trenches, at Farm Trench, Elbe Trench, and the junction of Fell and Felon with Epte Trench, as soon as the Brigade had established itself in them. " A " Company, attached to 169 Brigade, was to construct strong points in the German line and to consolidate a maze of trenches called " The Quadrilateral "; one platoon (2nd Lieut. C. H. Simpson) was attached to the London Rifle Brigade, one platoon (2nd Lieut. E. T. Andrews) to the Queen's Westminsters, and two platoons (2nd Lieuts. P. B. Bass and G. S. Arthur) to the Queen Victoria Rifles. Three platoons of " B " Company (Captain H. Caldecutt), with one platoon of " D," were attached to 167 Brigade, in reserve ; of these, two platoons (2nd Lieuts.

F. A. Davies and W. F. Smith) were to fix name boards and direction boards in the captured trenches ; one platoon (2nd Lieut. H. W. Glendinning) was to remove the barricades on the Hebuterne-Bucquoy road, and one platoon (2nd Lieut. J. D. Salmon) was to remove the barricades on the Hebuterne-Gommecourt road and throw three bridges over trenches. The remaining three platoons of " D " Company were in Divisional reserve at Souastre, and the specialist platoon of " B " Company at Henu.

On July 1st the great battle of the Somme commenced. The attack at Gommecourt, which was at the northern extremity of the long battle line, had been anticipated by the enemy, who had concentrated a large number of guns to counter it. Zero hour was 7-30 a.m. The enemy having received information of the time of the forth-coming attack, put down a heavy barrage earlier in the morning, causing numerous casualties in the assembly trenches. The attack of the Division was brilliantly carried out with great determination, the battle lasting the whole day, but it failed from a variety of causes, the chief of which was the severity of the enemy's artillery barrage, and to a lesser extent machine gun fire from the flanks, which prevented grenades and ammunition being carried across "No Man's Land."

" A " Company of the Cheshires went over by platoons in the third wave and commenced the construction of a strong point. The enemy, however, by intense bombing, drove the infantry back, and the Company had to abandon its task, discard its tools, and fight. After it had contributed its full share to a very glorious and heroic resistance against superior numbers, it was compelled to retire to the old front line at dusk, having lost four Officers and 113 other ranks. The following description, given by Corporal L. Ratcliffe, M.M., furnishes a graphic account of the fighting :—

> "We were told off to assist the Queen's Westminsters ("B" Company) in consolidating the right hand bottom corner of the Quadrilateral. We

went over after the Machine Guns at about 7·45 a.m. We got to the second line without stopping, but here we found they were fighting and there were many Germans on our right. Some men were put on to dig a trench here, but I was not required, so I observed for a Lewis Gunner of the Queen's Westminsters, and we fired at the Germans on our right for about 20 minutes. Then the Lewis Gunner was sniped and a bullet passed through my sleeve. A Sergt.-Major of the Queen's Westminsters (a D.C.M.) said: 'Come along this trench,' so we advanced to the German third line. I carried the Lewis Gun, Mugan carried the magazines. He said the Cheshires were to come too. He asked for Lewis Gunners and Bombers. We got there and our men were building a firestep in the communication trench facing right and the order came 'Stand to,' so we had to stop digging. Then a Queen Victoria Rifle's Officer came and asked me to place my gun on the right, to relieve the men standing to. I stayed there for about 1½ hours and enfiladed the Germans, who were in their third line on our right. I used six magazines. Then the Queen Victoria Rifle's Officer came and asked me to place my gun to command the German third line on the right, and as nobody came along the trench, I did not need to fire. After a time a man came to help me as Mugan was wounded. Several men were wounded here by hostile machine gun fire. A L/Corpl. and a No. 2 came along with a Lewis Gun, so I handed over my gun and 4 magazines to him. I then built him an emplacement facing right, and when it was finished, as there was so much fighting, I went back to get magazines. I passed magazines and bombs till they were finished, and some time afterwards we were told to go back to the second line, which we manned for about 15 minutes. Then we got on the parados and got the order to get to the first line, down the communication trench. We lost a great many here and got into the first line trench and manned it. We got in two traverses and blocked the trenches at each end and at the communication trench. We still got casualties so we made a parapet out of the German parapet and lay with our feet towards the wire. We then decided that the wounded should crawl through the wire, which they did. We thought we were the last men in, so we got into a shell hole in the wire. About 5 o'clock we heard the Germans bombing the dugouts, and before it was dusk we saw Germans come out and take in wounded."

"C" Company awaited orders in the reserve trenches; one platoon was ordered to reinforce the London Scottish, but on reaching the German wire this order was countermanded by the Officer on the spot in charge of the infantry and it rejoined the rest of the Company. "C" Company's casualties amounted to one Officer and 22 other ranks. The two platoons of "B" Company, for marking the trenches, attempted to go across, but

2nd Lieut. F. A. Davies on mounting the parapet was immediately killed, and the fire was so heavy and the situation so doubtful that they were ordered to stand fast. One of the barricades on the Bucquoy road was removed by another platoon, but the shell fire was so intense that no further work could with any advantage be carried out. The other platoon under 2nd Lieut. J. D. Salmon destroyed the barricades on the Gommecourt road with gun cotton, and threw their bridges across the trenches, brilliantly completing its task in its entirety. The casualties of the three platoons of " B " Company and one of " D " Company were one Officer and 37 other ranks.

The total casualties sustained by the Battalion were 6 Officers and 197 other ranks.

	Officers.	Other Ranks.
Killed	1	13
Wounded	3	98
Missing	2	77
Died of Wounds	–	9
	6	197

Of the missing, two Officers (2nd Lieuts. P. B. Bass and G. S. Arthur) were known to have been killed, and of the 77 other ranks the deaths of 30 were officially accepted, and 23 were known to have been wounded.

This battle, known as the battle of Gommecourt, was the first the 56th Division had taken part in, and the fine qualities they showed on this occasion earned for them a reputation as a fighting Division, a reputation which they not only upheld, but added to, in the many actions in which they subsequently took part.

The casualties of the Division were very heavy, amounting to 4,202.

The following messages from the Corps and Divisional Commanders were issued after the battle :—

Third Army No. S.G.R. 46/2. 56th Division, S.G. 121/96.
VIIth Corps G.C.R. 233/162.
General Officer Commanding,
   Third Army.
O.A.D. 64.

The Commander-in-Chief directs me to confirm in writing the verbal message delivered by an A.D.C. to General Snow, conveying his appreciation of the gallant efforts made at Gommecourt on the 1st and 2nd July, by the 26th and 56th Division of the VIIth Corps.

While deeply deploring the losses suffered by these Divisions, he is glad to be able to assure them that their vigorous and well-sustained attack has proved of material assistance to the success of the general plan of operations.

(Signed) L. E. KIGGELL, Lieut. General,
13th July, 1916. Chief of the General Staff.

VIIth Corps G.C.R. 237/140. 56th Division, S.G. 121/19.
56th Division.

The Corps Commander wishes to congratulate all ranks of the 56th Division on the way in which they took the German trenches and held them by pure grit and pluck for so long in very adverse circumstances.

Although Gommecourt has not fallen into our hands, the purpose of the attack which was mainly to contain and kill Germans was accomplished, thanks to a great extent to the tenacity of the 56th Division.

(Signed) F. LYON, Brigadier General,
3rd July, 1916. General Staff, VIIth Corps.

Forwarded. The General Officer commanding the 56th Division wishes all ranks to know how proud he is of the splendid way in which they captured the German trenches, and of the way they held on to them until all their ammunition and grenades were exhausted.

He is satisfied that the main task of the Division in containing and killing Germans was most thoroughly accomplished.

(Signed) J. BRIND, Lieut. Colonel,
H.Q., 56th Division. General Staff.
3rd July, 1916.

The G.O.C. Division in his report on the battle called particular attention to the following :—" The steady advance and determined resistance offered by the five assaulting Battalions, the 5th Londons (London Rifle Brigade), 9th Londons (Queen Victoria Rifles), 12th Londons (Rangers), 14th Londons (London Scottish), and 16th Londons (Queen's Westminsters), with the small parties of the 2/1st and 2/2nd London Field Companies R.E., and of the 1/5th Cheshire Regiment (Pioneers) attached to them."

After the battle the Companies returned to Souastre for re-organization and re-inforcements. The remainder of the month was spent in the same area, an additional piece of the line in front of Fonquevillers being taken over.

During this period the specialist platoon of " C " Company were engaged in the construction of new Brigade Head Quarter dug-outs at Sailly. These were of a very elaborate nature and were constructed of large " elephant " shelters sunk deep, with a strong covering of trees, bricks and earth. The following letter was received by the Commanding Officer regarding this work :—

> O. C., 1/5th Cheshire Regiment.
>
> Will you please accept to yourself and convey to the Platoon of the Battalion under your command which executed the work, my great appreciation of the speed and skill with which the Brigade Head Quarter's Dug-outs at Sailly have been constructed.
>
> The benefits will not unfortunately accrue to this Brigade, but to all Brigades succeeding us in this line, your good work will undoubtedly prove a real boon.
>
> G. S. LOCK, Brigadier General,
> 16/8/16. Commanding 168th Infantry Brigade.

On August 20th the whole Division moved back for rest and training, preparatory to taking further part in the great battle of the Somme, which was still raging. The Battalion marched to Doullens on the 20th, to Hiermont on the 22nd, and to St. Riquier on the 23rd, where it went into comfortable billets, and immediately commenced carrying out an intensive scheme of Pioneer training which subsequently proved of the utmost value during the succeeding operations. Whilst at this village the Battalion made its first acquaintance with tanks.

In the presence of High Command of the Allies, Marshall Joffre being present amongst others, a demonstration was given of the capabilities of these engines of warfare over trenches and other obstacles which had been prepared by the Battalion.

At the beginning of September the Division was ordered to join the XIV. Corps of the 4th Army, and on September 4th the Battalion entrained for Corbie, where it arrived the same night, in pouring rain, and went into billets. The following day it marched to the Citadel, where it went into huts, and on September 7th moved to Contour Copse, into bivouacs.

The Division captured Leuze Wood the same day, and the following night the Battalion went up to dig a communication trench up to this wood across what was known as "the Valley of Death." The journey up to the work was unhappy, several casualties being caused by shell fire during a rest at Brigade Head Quarters, for the purpose of obtaining guides, and the march across the recently fought over battle ground gave one a vivid impression, even in the dark, of the severity of the fighting On arrival at the site of work the trench was soon marked out, it being more a matter of joining up shell holes, as the whole of the ground was pock-marked with them. The trench, which ran up a steep slope, was partly earth and partly chalk, and during the work an uncomfortable time was experienced owing to hostile shell fire, at times almost amounting to barrage fire, seven men being killed and twelve wounded, this particular spot being a favourite target for hostile gunners. The trench was completed and a return made to camp, which was reached just before dawn.

On September 14th the Battalion moved forward to the Bois de Favier and bivouacked in trenches, Head Quarters being in an old enemy dressing station. On the slope just in front were some French 75's and an old French howitzer, the excitement of the French gunners, the beautiful working of the 75's, and the jumping antics of the old howitzer caused endless amusement.

On September 16th new fire trenches were dug and a communication trench, and on the following night a further new fire trench was commenced by " C " Company, and completed by " D " Company on the 18th. The latter trench was called Cheshire trench. These trenches were advanced fire trenches, to enable the infantry to get closer to their objective, Combles.

On September 19th the whole Battalion was employed in digging a new fire trench, right in front of the infantry, parallel to Bouleaux Wood, which was held by the enemy.

The following is an extract from 168 Brigade Order No. 29, of 19th September, 1916 :—

1. The 5th Division are now established on a line from T.21.b.0.9. T.15.d.0.4. T.15.b.5.0. T.9.d.5.2.
2. The front line held by this Brigade will be pushed forward to-night by digging a new trench from appx T.21.b.0.4. to Middle Copse and thence to junction of tramline and road at T.15.d.7.7.
3. This trench will be dug by the Cheshire Regiment (Pioneers) and will be occupied by parties of the London Scottish before dawn on the 20th inst.
4. London Scottish will find the covering party for to-night's digging and will be in position by 9 p.m. at the latest.
5. . . . .
6. Four Company Commanders and 8 O.R's of Cheshires will meet B.M. 168 Inf. Brigade at Brigade H.Q., Angle Wood, at 5-45 p.m., and go forward to tape out the trench line. This party will probably move out to Middle Copse at 7-45 p.m.

In accordance with these orders, the four Company Commanders, Captains E. J. Bairstow, H. N. Hignett, T. L. C. Heald, and O. Johnson, went on in advance and, with Captain P. Neame, V.C. (the Brigade Major), taped out the trench as soon as it was dusk. The Battalion, under Major W. A. V.

Aeroplane Photograph of Gropi Trench.

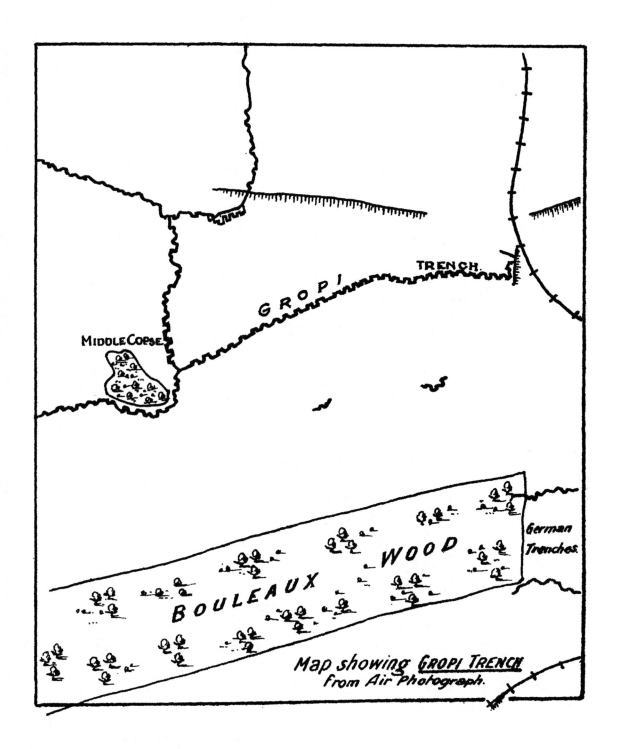

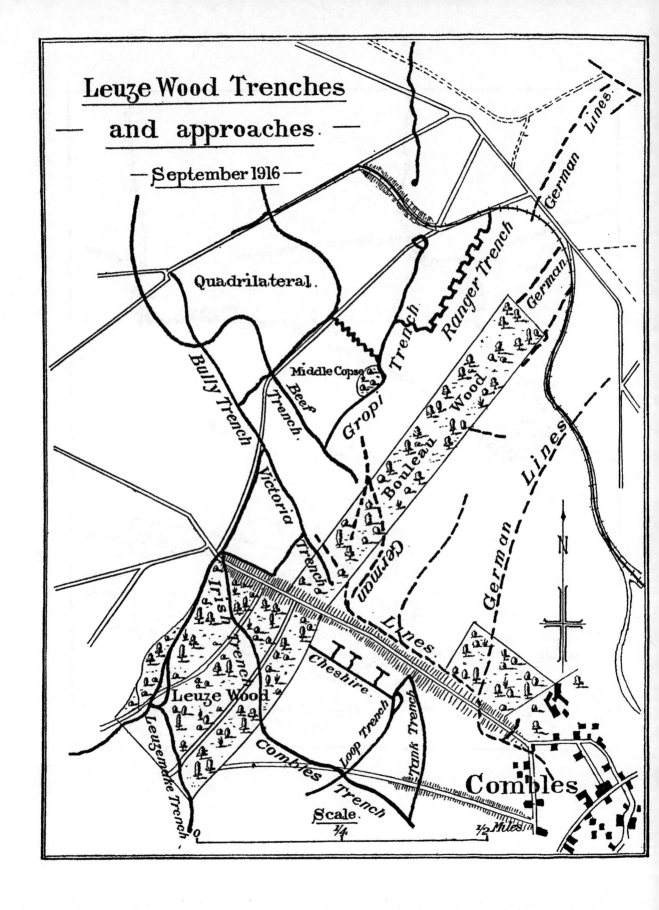

Churton, followed, and after a difficult march in pitch darkness reached Leuze Wood, where guides were to have been met. These, however, failed to put in an appearance, but after a short advance the Company Commanders met the Battalion and guided the Companies to their work. During the progress of the work the enemy was quiet, and the complete trench, some 1,000 yards long, was entirely completed during the night, with only one casualty, a most remarkable performance considering that the enemy were close by in Bouleaux Wood. This trench was named " Gropi " trench as a compliment to the Battalion, " Gropi " being the code name of the unit, a combination of the words Groves, the Commanding Officer, and pioneer.

The following congratulatory order was sent to the Division by the XIV. Corps Commander :—

Secret.
XIVth Corps G. 203/6.
56th Division.

    The Corps Commander has directed me to forward to you the attached Photograph, and draw your attention to the Trench marked in Red, which he considers is a perfect example of a Battle Trench dug in close proximity to the enemy and reflects the greatest credit on the unit which constructed it. He considers that the digging of all divisions with a view to the forthcoming operations is most satisfactory, but the air photographs have shown no trench in which such careful arrangements have been made for the security of the garrisons.

    (Signed) F. GATHORNE HARDY, Brigadier General,
23rd Sept., 1916.   General Staff, XIVth Corps.

The photograph is that of Gropi trench.

During the following days strong points were pushed out from Gropi trench, and a new switch trench on the easterly side was dug and named Ranger trench.

On the night of the 21st " B " Company, whilst working north of Bouleaux Wood, had four Officers wounded, one of whom, 2nd Lieut. W. F. Smith, subsequently died of his wounds, and a large shell burst in the midst of a platoon of " D " Company as they were forming up to come home after work near Wedge Wood, killing six and wounding seven, of whom three, including Company Sergeant-Major F. Sweeney, died of their wounds.

On the 25th September the 168 Brigade attacked from Ranger and Gropi trenches, " C " Company constructing strong points at night and consolidating their gains.

On the 26th the Division attacked in conjunction with the French, on their right, and captured Combles. By a happy coincidence the number of the French Division attacking was the 56th, and the joint entry of the two 56th Divisions into what remained of the village was the subject of a cartoon in *Punch*, which was subsequently adopted by the Division as its Christmas Card for 1916.

On September 27th the Battalion moved back to Méaulte, to the Sandpits, but on the 30th went up to the line again to Montauban, relieving the 11th Leicester Regiment (Pioneers) and the 4th Coldstream Guards (Pioneers), as the Division was again going to attack.

The scheme of operations was an attack on the Brown Line at Le Transloy, all the Companies being engaged in digging strong points and new assembly trenches.

On October 11th the Division, being pretty well exhausted, was withdrawn from the line and returned to the neighbourhood of Picquigny to rest. The Cheshires, however, only went back to the Citadel and were engaged on work for the Corps for a week, before they entrained and moved to Condé Folie. The Battalion had had a very strenuous time during the five weeks it had been engaged on the Somme. The bivouacking in the open, nightly marches up to work, frequently under heavy shell fire, and work in the most forward and exposed positions, had put a heavy strain on all ranks, but the dangers and discomforts were endured with exemplary cheerfulness and all thoroughly deserved their much needed rest.

The casualties during the Somme Battle were :—

	Officers.	Other Ranks.
Killed	1	47
Wounded	7	120
	8	167

During the operations a party from "A" Company had been attached to the Divisional Signal Company.

The following is an extract from a letter received by the Colonel :—

Dear Colonel Groves,

I wish to thank you on the return of the detachment of Cheshires which have been with me for the past month for your kindness in arranging this. I can only say their work without exception has been thoroughly carried out and deliberately done, and particularly when the working parties have been under shell fire.

Yours sincerely,
GORDON KENNARD, Major R.E.,
O/c. Signals, 56th Div.

On leaving the 4th Army the following message was sent by General Sir H. Rawlinson :—

56th Division.   Fourth Army No. G.S. 334.

I desire to place on record my appreciation of the work that was carried out by the 56th Division during the Battle of the Somme. The successful operations in the neighbourhood of Bouleaux and Leuze Woods, together with the capture of Combles between 9th and 27th September, were feats of arms deserving of the highest praise, and I congratulate the Division on the gallantry, perseverance and endurance displayed by all ranks.

When after only two days' rest the Division was again called upon to go into the line, they displayed a fine spirit of determination which deserved success.

The work of the Divisional Artillery in supporting the infantry attacks and in establishing barrages under difficult circumstances was satisfactory, and shows that a high standard of efficiency has been reached.

The enterprise and hard work which the Division has shown in sapping forward and constructing trenches under fire has been a noticeable feature in the operations, and I specially congratulate the Infantry on the progress they made in this manner at Bouleaux Wood.

It is a matter of regret to me that this fine Division has now left the Fourth Army, but I trust that at some future time I may again find them under my command.

RAWLINSON, General,
H.Q., Fourth Army.   Commanding Fouth Army.
27th October, 1916.

On October 21st the Battalion marched to Hallencourt, and on the 24th entrained at Pont Remy, where Captain E. S. Bourne of the Battalion was R.T.O., detraining the following morning at Cornet Malo, and on the 28th they marched to Laventie, where they relieved the 1/5th Duke of Cornwall's Light Infantry, the Pioneer Battalion of the 66th Division.

The Division, who were now in the XI. Corps of the 1st Army, had taken over an extensive sector in front of the Aubers Ridge. The trenches, or rather breastworks, were in poor condition and very wet, all the ground in the area being very low lying. An intricate system of drainage had been carried out right up to the front line trenches and required continual attention. "B" Company took over this work, the men being supplied with "Gum boots, thigh," as they had to work nearly all the time in water. The number of drains to be looked after was immense, these gradually converging into a large cross drain called the "Blue Nile," and thence into the river Lys. "D" Company marched to Croix Barbée, taking over the work in the Neuve Chapelle Sector, "A" and "C" Companies taking over the work in the left and centre sectors. Although Laventie was within easy field gun range of the German lines, there were plenty of civilians in the town, which was not at that period shelled. As it was probable that the Battalion would spend the winter in the town, steps were taken to put the billets into good repair and to arrange recreation for the men.

The Battalion was fortunate in being in possession of the Parish School, a large set of buildings which accommodated the Quartermaster's Stores, Tailor's, Shoemaker's and Butcher's Shops, together with the Head Quarter Pioneer Workshop and some excellently constructed Cook Houses. A Canteen and Boxing Hall were established on the premises, which proved a great source of enjoyment to the men. A portion of the school was fitted up as a Church by Colonel Groves, at some considerable expense. The Chaplain-General to the Forces held a confirmation here on December 12th, 1916, at which nearly 200 men from the Division were confirmed. Daily services were held at this Church by the Divisional Chaplain throughout the winter. In addition to putting their own billets into order, the Battalion erected a large number of splendid cook houses for the use of all troops occupying the town, which added very greatly to their comfort.

A series of Divisional Football and Boxing Competitions were arranged, and several notable fights took place in the boxing ring, which was always crowded as there were several other Battalions in the town. At Christmas, festivities were arranged and extra fare procured from the well stocked shops of Estaires. Owing to the impossibility of securing turkeys, and as roast beef was a daily ration, a supply of Belgian hares was purchased. These arrived at the stores alive, and were killed by the cooks, who made them into a savoury stew for the dinners, which were held by Companies in their respective billets.

The Battalion Football XI. started well in the Divisional Association Football Competition, for a cup presented by Lieut.-General Sir Amyatt Hull, K.C.B., defeating the 416th Edinburgh Field Company by four goals to three, and the 2/1st

London Field Company by ten goals to nil in the first and second rounds. The team showed excellent form, which promised well for the matches to be played in the New Year.

The year ended with a sudden spell of frost and snow, which lasted well into February and considerably interfered with work in the line.

CHAPTER IV.

1917.

ARRAS : YPRES : CAMBRAI.

THE year opened with the Battalion at Laventie, and work was much interfered with by a prolonged spell of very severe frost, which was followed by a heavy downfall of snow and a subsequent thaw, which played havoc with the ditches and trenches in the sector. On February 13th Field Marshal Sir Douglas Haig visited the Division, and the Battalion was one of the Units of the Division singled out for his inspection, which took the form of a march past in fours on the Lestrem—la Gorgue road.

The Battalion's Football XI. continued its victorious career by defeating the 2/2nd London Field Company by sixteen goals to nil, and in the semi-final the 280th Brigade R.F.A. by five goals to nil. The final, which was played at Merville before a large crowd, was a fine and clean game against the 2/3rd London Field Ambulance. The Cheshire's team proved too speedy for the "thirds," and won comfortably by four goals to one, the cup being presented by General Sir Amyatt Hull to Sergt. F. Moss at the conclusion of the game, medals being subsequently presented to the team by him at Arras.

The winning team was :—Goal, Lance-Corpl. Radley ; backs, Corpl. Blease, Sergt. Kay ; half-backs, Pte. Moss, Sergt. F. Moss, Corpl. J. White ; forwards, Corpl. A. Davies, Lance-Corpl. Jones, Sergt. T. Kelly, Pte. A. Furness, Lance-Corpl. A. Johnson.

On March 3rd the Battalion received orders to leave the Division (which went back for a rest) and to join the XVIII. Corps for special work at Arras. They marched from Laventie to Merville, where they billeted for the night, and the following morning embussed for Arras, in a snowstorm. Arras was not reached until after dark, as the convoy had to wait outside, near Etrun, until dark, the approach to the town being visible in daylight from the German lines on Vimy Ridge. On arrival they went into billets between the Cathedral and the Canal, Head Quarters being in the Rue de Bethlehem. The work carried out for the Corps was all of a nature preparatory to an offensive, all the forward roads in St. Sauveur being cleared of barricades and repaired, an additional level crossing also being constructed across the railway metals at the station. After a fortnight's work for the Corps, the Battalion rejoined the 56th Division, which had taken over the Beaurains Sector under the VII. Corps, and moved into fresh billets on the south of the town at Hôpital Auxiliaire, a very large building which accommodated the whole Battalion. On the 17th it was found that the enemy had evacuated his trenches west of Beaurains and had retired to a line Telegraph Hill—Neuville-Vitasse, about 2,000 yards east of his old line, and the same night "A" and "B" Companies joined up the old English and German lines by means of two communication trenches across the old No Man's Land. Work was now concentrated on the forward roads, which were badly cut up by shell fire, to enable the artillery to get forward. During this work 2nd Lieut. N. P. Sandiford was killed by an anti-aircraft shell, which burst on reaching the ground, two other officers standing with him having a miraculous escape.

Guns and troops began to pour into Arras, and the Hôpital Auxiliaire became a terribly noisy spot, as the adjoining park and citadel was stiff with guns of all sorts and sizes.

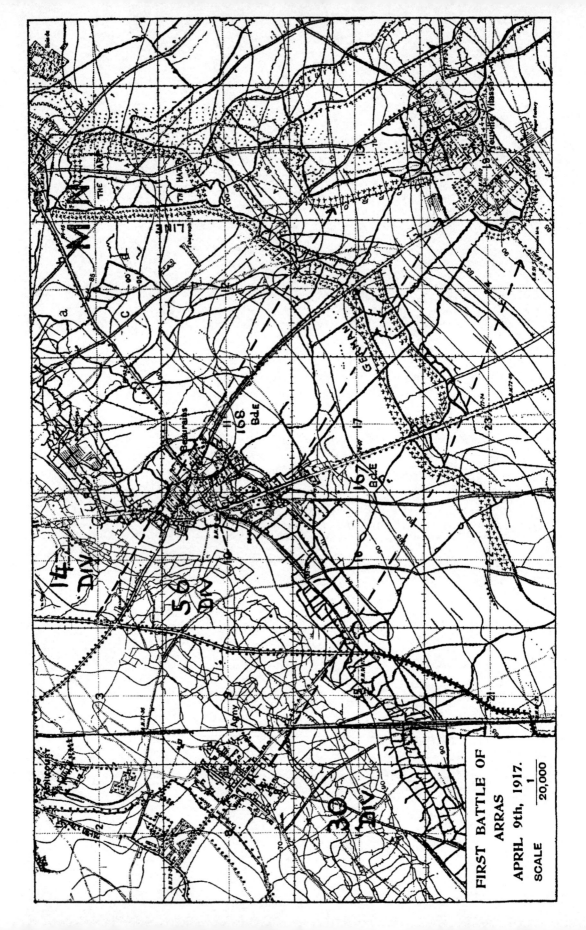

At the beginning of April news was received from England that Sir T. H. Marshall, C.B., V.D., the Honorary Colonel of the Battalion, had died on March 29th.

On April 7th, in view of the forthcoming operations, eight Officers and 107 other ranks proceeded to Gouy to join the Divisional surplus personnel Battalion, which was concentrating at Le Souich, and " C " Company moved the same day to Beaurains, for attachment to 167 Brigade. On the following day the remainder of the Battalion moved to take up its battle positions in some trenches south-east of Agny.

The objective of the attack, which was to be made by the First and Third Armies, was to break through the enemy's defences, which consisted of the famous Hindenburg Line. The VII. Corps was to attack on the right of and simultaneously with the VI. Corps. The frontage allotted to the 56th Division was that to the north-west of Neuville Vitasse, and the line of attack ran in a south-easterly direction—167 Brigade being on the right and 168 Brigade on the left, with 169 Brigade in reserve.

On the 9th the attack was made in atrocious weather, and proved highly successful, the Division capturing Neuville Vitasse. The same day " A " Company cleared the road through Achicourt, which was hopelessly blocked owing to an ammunition convoy having been blown up, through some heavy hostile shelling. " D " Company cleared the road to Neuville Vitasse, and " C " Company were employed in making strong points and consolidating a new advanced line. The advance continued rapidly, the Division capturing Heninel and Wancourt Tower, and during the next two days heavy work was put in clearing the forward roads to Henin and Wancourt, Head Quarters moving forward to the old German second line of trenches.

On the 19th the Division was relieved by the 30th Division, and moved back to the Souastre area, the Cheshires being once again billeted in that village and being joined there by their surplus personnel. After ten days' rest the Division again took over a Sector east of Arras, the Battalion relieving the 4th Gordon Highlanders (Pioneers). Two Companies went forward for work with two Brigades in the line, the other two Companies being in Arras. Head Quarters were in Rue de Rapporteurs.

The British line in the Sector taken over by the Division covered the Arras—Cambrai road to the Cojeul River, east of Guemappe, the enemy holding a line west of Bois du Sart, Bois du Vert, and the St. Rohart Factory. The two forward Companies of the Battalion bivouacked in some old trenches in front of Tilloy Wood. From here they had an unpleasant march each night to the neighbourhood of Cavalry Farm. The journey took about one-and-a-half hours, and, after crossing the Wancourt Line, was frequently interrupted owing to heavy shell fire. As the country was very open it was not easy to find the way in the dark, and the Royal Engineers fixed an acetylene lamp on a high pole at the end of Telegraph Ridge, to act as a beacon for the troops. When returning this lamp represented safety, as there was no shelling beyond it, except on one occasion, when one fell close by the camp and wounded one man.

On May 3rd, at 3-45 a.m., a simultaneous attack was made by the Fifth, Third and First Armies, the objective of the attack being the high ground east of the Bois du Sart, Bois du Vert, St. Rohart, and Cherisy. The 56th Division attacked with the 3rd Division on its left and the 14th Division on its right, the attack being carried out by the 167 and 169 Brigades. The attack was not successful as a whole, although the Division captured Cavalry Farm, which the enemy recaptured in the evening by a counter-attack. During the succeeding fortnight the Division was engaged in minor operations around Cavalry Farm and Tool Trench, and during this period the forward Companies of the Battalion had a strenuous time in consolidating

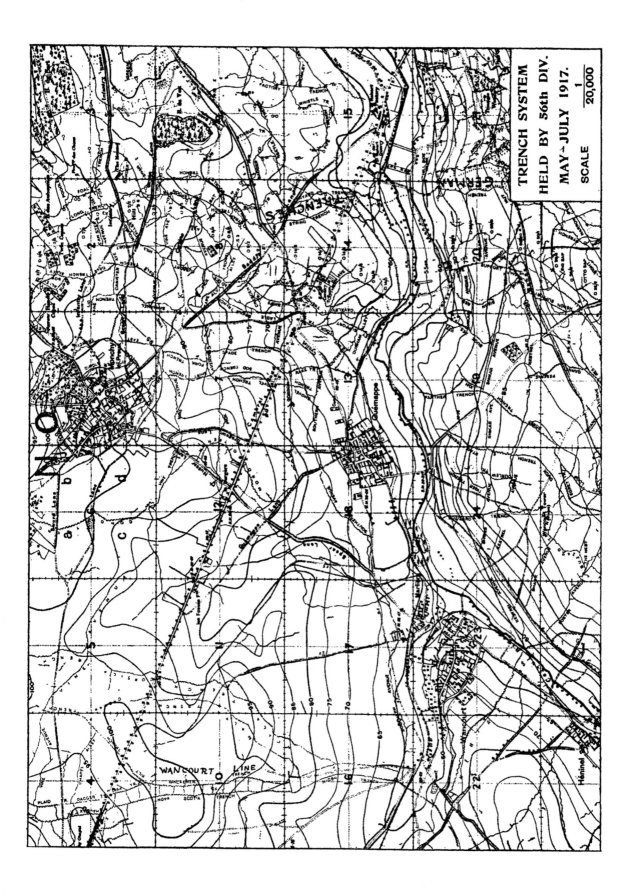

and improving the advanced trenches, and their communications. The two Companies in Arras were employed in repairing the Arras—Cambrai road, which had been badly damaged by shell fire.

A large ammunition dump exploded close to the Battalion's billets in Arras, which caused several casualties to troops in the neighbourhood, and kept burning for a considerable time, great anxiety being felt as to the fate of an adjoining gas shell dump, which luckily remained unaffected. The town was regularly shelled at a long range by high velocity guns, and a shell from one of these landed in Battalion Head Quarters. Several men had miraculous escapes, but only two casualties were caused, one of which proved fatal. The shell passed through an upper room full of men before bursting on the junction of the wall and floor and exploding in a downward direction. As a result, a fire owing to the presence of some inflamatory chemicals in an adjoining room was narrowly averted. On May 17th, Captain J. B. Armitage was killed by a shell whilst working in the forward area.

On May 20th the Division was relieved by the 37th Division, and on May 26th the Battalion marched back to Gouves, having been relieved by the 9th North Staffordshire Regiment. After a rest of only five days, two Companies were again sent to Arras for work under the VI. Corps. On June 6th the Battalion left Gouves and marched to bivouacs near Telegraph Hill, the Division having taken over the Sector covering the Cambrai Road, across the Cojeul River, to the high ground east of Wancourt. Two Companies bivouacked in the Wancourt line. Work was carried out in the left Sector on improving and deepening Gordon Alley, a long communication trench to the front line, digging a new communication trench called Southern Avenue, and remaking Spade and Rake trenches, whilst in the right Sector work was chiefly concentrated on Shikar Avenue and

Egret Lion and Panther Trenches. On the night of the 18th/19th, " A " Company, assisted by parties of Infantry, commenced to dig and wire four new strong posts in advance of the front line south of the river. These were completed and occupied by the Infantry the following night, and another new trench was dug behind them as a support trench, together with a sap joining the new trench with the old front line, Ape Trench, both of which were also wired.

On July 3rd the Battalion left the forward area and marched to Gouy, and the following day to Grand Rullecourt, where the Division had assembled for rest and training, preparatory to taking part in forthcoming operations at Ypres. During the Battalions stay in this Village training was carried out in the Chateau Park, which afforded facilities for the purpose.

On July 6th the Battalion was honoured by H.R.H. the Prince of Wales being gazetted as their Honorary Colonel.

On July 8th a Church parade had been arranged, at which their Majesties the King and Queen were to have been present, but rain came down in such torrents on the Sunday morning that the parade was cancelled, to the great disappointment of all.

On July 14th, Battalion Sports were held in the Chateau Grounds, a long and varied programme of events having been arranged. In addition to the individual contests, a group competition was arranged, whereby the first, second and third in each event counted so many points for their respective groups. In order to carry this out the Battalion was divided into five groups, Head Quarters and Transport, and the four Companies. The preliminary heats had been run off under Company arrangements and orders had been issued that every man in the Battalion was to take part in these, so that they should not be confined only to expert runners. This system proved highly successful and created great competition between the various groups. A large number of guests, including the Divisional Commander, were present, and a most enjoyable afternoon was spent under ideal weather conditions. The group competition was easily won by Head Quarters.

On July 22nd the Battalion marched to Bouquemaison, and the following day entrained for Wizernes, to join the V. Corps. On reaching their destination they marched to Longueness and subsequently to Ganspette, some 10 miles from St. Omer. In this neighbourhood the Division was in army reserve and hard training was carried out, but it was much interrupted by the heavy rain, which persistently fell and interfered so much with the offensive.

On August 6th the Battalion marched to Watten Station and moved by train to Wippenhoek, the transport proceeding by road. On arrival, they were billeted in tents and huts at Connaught Camp. On the 12th a further advance was made to Ouderdom, quarters being found in Ottawa Camp. From here "A" Company was detached for special advanced light railway work, taking over from a Company of the 11th South Lancashires. On the 14th the Battalion moved to Chateau Segard and took over the bivouacs of the 5th Royal Sussex Regiment. Their arrival at this spot was exciting, as three large high velocity shells arrived in the camp just when they had marched in, one was a "dud" and landed right on the footpath running through the camp, another landed by the Quartermaster's Stores, close to where three Officers, including the Quartermaster, were standing, but being an armour piercing shell it sank deep into the ground before exploding. The explosion knocked over all three Officers, who miraculously found themselves untouched on the edge of the crater ; it also pushed over the stores hut, but the only casualties were four men slightly wounded. The third shell went over the camp, doing no damage. These shells were evidently meant for a Battery of 6 inch Naval guns, about 200 yards behind the camp, whose bark was a continual source of annoyance during our stay here.

On the same day the Division took over the Glencorse Copse Sector, and on the 16th an attack was made on Glencorse Copse and Polygon Wood, " C " Company and " D " Company being attached to the 167 and 169 Brigades, and moving up to the Halfway House for the purpose. The attack was not a success, but at night " B," " C " and " D " Companies were all employed in carrying material, and constructing and wiring strong points for the infantry, on the new line they had reached. The night was a terrible one, the ground being so cut up by shell fire and the mud so deep and tenacious that movement was almost impossible, and the shelling was so intense that little constructional work was feasible. The Companies returned in the early morning quite exhausted.

The Division, owing to the number of casualties it had sustained in the attack, was withdrawn, being relieved by the 14th Division on the night of 17th/18th. On the 18th the Battalion (less " A " Company) moved back to Connaught Camp.

The casualties of the Battalion during its short stay at Ypres were :—Officers killed, 2nd Lieut. F. Newton ; died of wounds, 2nd Lieut. K. D. Rees ; wounded, 2nd Lieut. H. S. Burt ; N.C.O's. and men, three killed and thirty-eight wounded.

On the 21st, " C " Company was detached and lent to the 14th Division, and " B " Company to the 47th Division. On August 26th, Head Quarters and " D " Company marched to Abeele and entrained for Watten, moving from there by road to billets at Ouest Mont. On the 29th the Division received orders to move into the 3rd Army, and " A," " B " and " C " Companies rejoined the same evening. On the 30th the Battalion left for Wizernes and proceeded by rail to Miraumont, subsequently marching to Bapaume, where they went under canvas. On September 4th the Division relieved the 3rd Division on the IV. Corps front, taking over the Lagnicourt—Morchies-Louverval Sector, a very extended front of 11,000 yards, and reported to be a quiet one. The Battalion relieved the 20th Bn. King's Royal Rifle Corps, " D " Company moving to Morchies in the left Sector, " A," " B " and " C " Companies to Beaumetz, for work on the centre and right Sectors; Head Quarters were in huts near Haplincourt, but after about a month's stay they moved forward to a new camp of Nissen huts, which they had erected for themselves at Lebucquiere. This area was part of that which had been evacuated by the enemy the previous winter and was absolutely devastated, the villages being mere shells and ruins. During September and October work was concentrated on the intermediate line, which was in only a partly constructed condition and in a bad state of repair, the front line being held by a series of posts. The enemy during this period was quiet, and there was little shelling of any back areas. At the beginning of November it soon became evident that something was brewing, as the Battalion was employed nightly, with two Field Companies of the 62nd Division, on widening the main Cambrai road, by corduroying the north side of the road from Beugny to Boursies. This work, which was pushed on with feverish haste, was completed on the 20th. On the 16th the Head Quarters of the 16th Bn. Royal Irish Rifles was billeted at our Head Quarters, by closing up, and for the first time news leaked out that an attack was impending. No additional camps had been constructed, no guns had registered, and the greatest secrecy had been maintained. On the 20th the attack was launched, the 56th Division on the extreme left of the attack making a feint, in which dummy tanks, dummy figures, and smoke screens were extensively used.

The attack of the Corps was a great success, the enemy being completely surprised and overwhelmed by the large numbers of tanks used. The line was advanced several kilometres, into a salient, the left hinge of which was the left Sector of the Division, at Lagnicourt, the right of the Division swinging to its left and capturing Tadpole Copse.

On the 21st, " A " and " B " Companies, who had moved up to Boursies, proceeded the same night to clear the main Cambrai road up to the Canal du Nord. There were two immense craters in the road, one in front of the enemy's support line, and the other in front of their reserve line; their trenches were also cut through the road. The craters were circumvented by laying a corduroy road round the north side. The work on the first crater was done so fast that material for the corduroying of the second crater was able to get past the first crater before daylight. This operation demanded the employment of a great amount of transport to bring up the logs required for the road, as no material of any kind was available on the spot. The whole of the work was under the superintendence of Major Gedge, R.E. By the 23rd the corduroying was completed and material got forward for the canal crossing. On the 24th all the Companies were engaged in consolidating the new defensive flank of the Division, and the same night, owing to the change in the tactical situation, the Division was transferred to the VI. Corps. The enemy by this time had been rushing up reserves of men and guns, the attack had been held up, and the action of the enemy became much more lively and aggressive, so much so that the Companies had to evacuate Boursies, which had become a shell trap. The Company's cook-house received a direct hit from a shell which killed the Battalion Sergeant Cook, " B " Company's tool Corporal, and one man, and wounded several others. One field cooker was completely put out of action, and the second considerably damaged.

As there was no need for secrecy any longer, canvas camps in the back areas sprang up like mushrooms and considerable

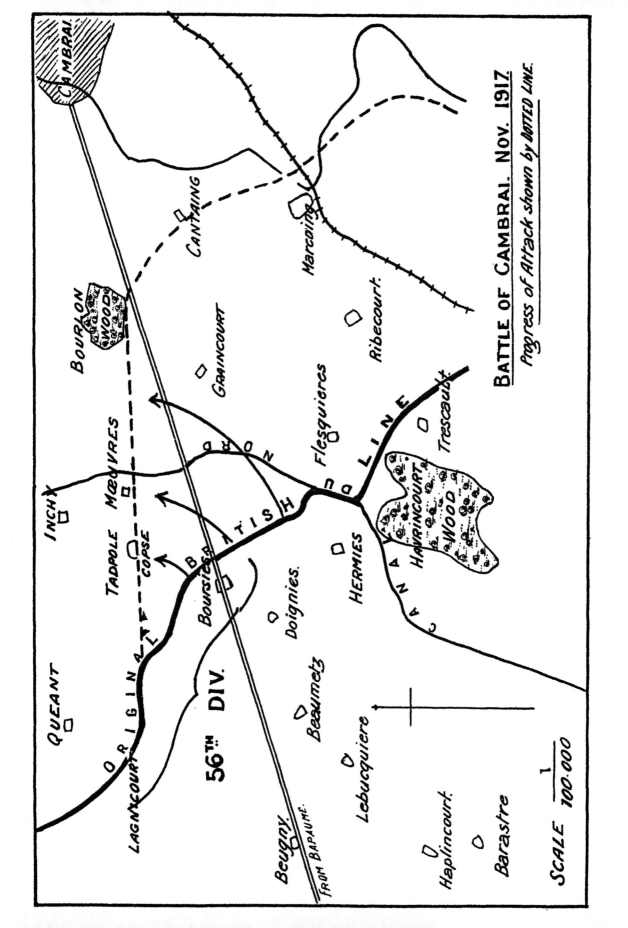

congestion of billets arose owing to the large numbers of troops pouring in. On November 30th orders were received for Battalion Head Quarters to move from Lebucquiere to Fremicourt,—their departure was hastened by the arrival of high velocity shells in the camp for the first time since its erection,—and for " A," " B " and " C " Companies to go under canvas at Lebucquiere.

No sooner had the camps been pitched, and Head Quarters moved, than a message came, ordering the three Companies to reinforce 169 Brigade, and " D " Company 168 Brigade. The three Companies immediately went up and took up a position in the old British front line, Lieut.-Col. Groves having his Head Quarters in Whiting Trench. On the morning of this day the enemy had launched a very heavy counter-attack on the north and south sides of the salient, with the object of breaking through and cutting off the troops in the salient itself. At this time the 2nd Division was on the right of the 56th Division, east of the Canal du Nord, and the 47th Division were on their right holding Bourlon Wood. These three Divisions beat off the enemy's frequent attacks in magnificent style, after some most stubborn and, at times, hand to hand fighting, at what was a most critical part in the British Line, and with the exception of the loss of a few advanced positions had maintained the line intact and inflicted enormous losses on the enemy. The Division, being exhausted after their ten days' continuous fighting, on the night of the 1st/2nd December was relieved by the 51st Division, the Cheshires handing over their trenches to the 4th Bn. Gordon Highlanders. " A " Company in particular had suffered severely in the line from enemy gas shells, having fifty casualties. The Companies, on relief, moved back to Lebucquiere, and the following day the Battalion entrained at Fremicourt and proceeded to Dainville, where they remained until the 5th. The Division having been transferred to the XIII. Corps and taking over the Sector just south of Vimy in front of Oppy and Gavrelle, the Battalion moved to St. Aubin on the 5th, and on the 7th to huts at Aubrey Camp, north of Arras. "A" Company remained with Head Quarters, but " B " and " C " Companies moved to bivouacs near Daylight Railhead, and " D " Company to trenches in Winter and Summer Lanes in the left Sector. Work was carried out on the trench system and was hindered to a very considerable extent by the weather, which was extremely cold, and by the frequent heavy falls of snow. On December 22nd Head Quarters and " A " Company moved from Aubrey Camp to billets at St. Catherine.

Christmas found the Battalion much scattered and bivouacking in about a foot of snow, so all festivities were postponed until the Battalion went out for a rest and suitable accommodation existed for celebrating the feast.

CHAPTER V.

1918.

ARRAS : CROISILLES : CANAL DU NORD.
ARMISTICE.

ON January 9th the Division went back for a rest and the Battalion moved to Bailleul aux Cornailles, the Companies proceeding by light railway from Roclincourt to Maroueil, and thence by broad guage to Tincques. The weather was bitterly cold and a blizzard greatly interfered with the move, the transport having a very trying time and only just getting through before the roads became almost impassable owing to the depth of snow. The postponed Christmas dinners were arranged in this village, rooms at three Estaminets being utilized for the purpose, each Company holding their dinner on separate days owing to the scarcity of accommodation. These passed off very successfully, the fare consisting of roast pork and plum pudding, the meat being obtained by buying live pigs from a local dealer. The transport and execution of these animals created considerable excitement amongst the inhabitants of the village, who seemed to look upon the killing of a pig as a great ceremony.

On January 22nd " A " and " B " Companies moved up to St. Catherine, just north of Arras, for work under the Corps, mining dugouts, and " C " and " D " followed them on the 31st.

On February 7th the Division again took over their old sector, and Battalion Head Quarters returned to its previous billets at St. Catherine, three Companies taking over their old bivouacs near Daylight Railhead. From now onwards it was evident that preparations were being made to meet a hostile attack. The trench system in the battle zone consisted of three distinct lines, with posts in advance, and during the next two months an enormous amount of wire was put out, the Battalion erecting at least twenty miles of double apron fence, so that by the end of March the whole of the battle front of the Division was a perfect maze of barbed wire running at all angles, to a very considerable depth. The value of this work was very apparent when the enemy made his great attack on March 28th.

During February the Battalion Football XI. had a series of hard matches in the Divisional Association Football Cup Competition. Against the Gunners in a preliminary round they played two drawn games, and were beaten in the second replay by one goal to none.

On February 21st, Lieut.-Col. J. E. G. Groves, C.M.G., T.D., who had proceeded to England on leave on January 21st, was struck off the strength of the Battalion, upon the report of a medical board, his health having suffered severely owing to the strain of his long service at the front. Major W. A. V. Churton, D.S.O., T.D., was appointed to command the Battalion, Captain N. B. Ellington, M.C., taking over the duties of second in command.

At the beginning of March a new establishment for Pioneer Battalions came into operation and the number of Companies was reduced from four to three, although the strength of the Battalion was only slightly reduced. In order to carry this out, " A " Company was split up and its personnel distributed amongst the other three Companies, " D " Company being renamed " A." The establishment figures were:—Officers 27, N.C.O's. and men 832, horses and mules 72, vehicles 29.

Lieut.-Col. W. A. V. Churton, D.S.O., T.D.

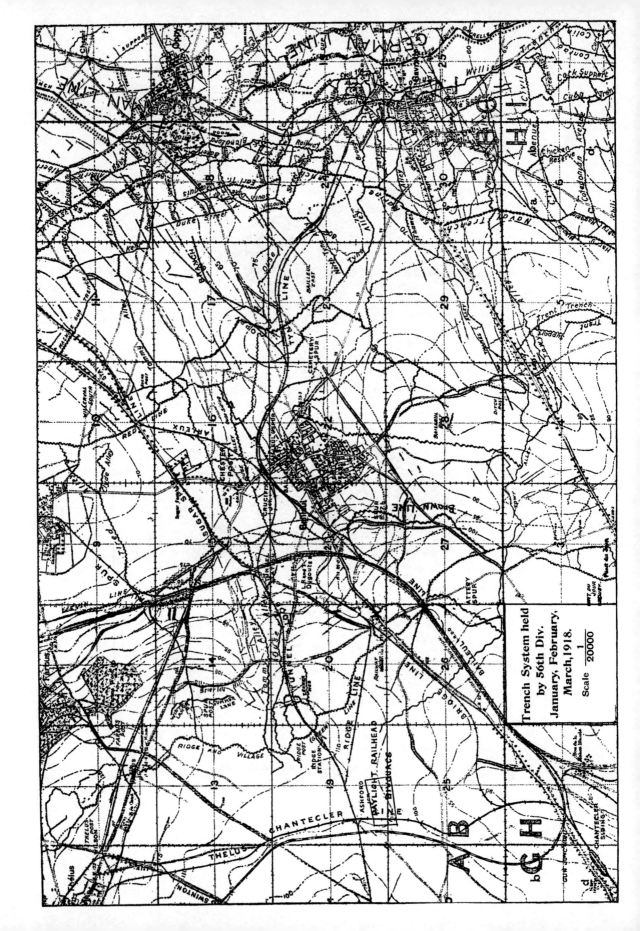

On March 12th orders were received that a special state of readiness for action should be observed, and the Battalion stood to arms daily at 5 a.m. On March 21st the enemy started a heavy bombardment along the front and on Arras, and during the next few days the situation became electrical. On the 27th a special reserve Brigade was formed in the Division, under Lieut.-Col. Mozley, D.S.O., the C.R.E., consisting of the Pioneer Battalion, the three Field Companies of Engineers, No. 176 Tunnelling Company, and the Divisional Employment Company. On the night of the 27th/28th the Companies took up their battle positions in support of the Infantry, two Platoons of " B " Company manning Railway Post and two Platoons Chester Post (named after the Battalion owing to it having been reconstructed by them). " C " Company garrisoned Ridge Post, and " A " Company occupied the Brown line at its southern end.

At 4 a.m. on the 28th the long expected attack was launched full on the Divisional front, commencing with an intense bombardment of gas and high explosive shells and followed by an avalanche of Infantry. Severe fighting took place all day, but in spite of repeated renewals of the enemy's attack the waves broke on the hard front of the 56th, who, fighting magnificently, and with great grit and determination, held the enemy in check and preserved their front intact, only a few advanced posts having been overwhelmed in the initial rush.

On the night of 28th/29th the two platoons of " B " Company from Chester Post reinforced the London Scottish in the front line. On the 29th no further attacks developed, the enemy having exhausted himself, and on the night of the 29th/30th the Division was relieved by the 4th Canadian Division, the Cheshires concentrating at St. Catherine. The Battalion's casualties during the battle were :—Captain E. S. Heron and fifteen other ranks killed, and thirty wounded.

This heavy German reverse had a great effect on the situation on the allied front, and the following extract from the war memories of General von Ludendorff shows how the battle affected the enemy's plans :—" The 17th Army had already attacked in the last days of March in the district of Arras, making its principal effort on the north bank of the Scarpe. It was to capture the decisive heights east and north of Arras, and the next day the 6th Army was to prolong the attack from about Lens and carry the high ground in that area. I attached the greatest importance to both these attacks. To have the high ground in our possession was bound to be decisive in any fighting in the plain of the Lys. In spite of employing extraordinary masses of artillery and ammunition the attack on both banks of the Scarpe was a failure, it fought under an unlucky star, only the 12th Division under General Lequis made good progress south of the stream, but this was not enough to influence the whole operation, apparently the artillery had not been sufficiently effective. G.H.Q. now abandoned the attack by the south wing of the 6th Army."

On March 31st the Battalion moved to Estree Cauchy, where they remained until April 6th, on which date they marched in pouring rain to St. Aubin, and the following night to the Ronville Caves, Arras, relieving the 107th (Pioneer) Battalion of the 1st Canadian Division, the transport moving to Dainville. Arras at this period was receiving a considerable amount of shelling daily, especially in the region of the station and the Caves, several British Batteries being in the Ronville district, and the Battalion's arrival there was by no means peaceful.

The Ronville and St. Sauveur Caves are among the wonders of Arras, being excavated out of the chalk and of great depth, their history dating back several centuries. The entrance to them was effected by means of a large number of shafts with steep steps. The caves, which were all named after Generals, *e.g.*, Wellington Cave, were lit by electric light and afforded accommodation for a very large number of troops. The passages in them were of great length and rather confusing. The main passage had a light railway line in it for trucks, but when these were used it was almost impossible for any one to pass, and when they got off the line, as they frequently did, they caused great congestion. One passage led into the main sewer of Arras, which was 10 feet high, built of brick, with a raised footpath on one side, and there were various exits from it into the town. To the east there was a long passage which led right up to the old front line trenches, a distance of some 1,200 yards. The caves were very damp and full of gritty dust and by no means healthy, and great care had to be exercised to prevent the inlet of any gas down the shafts, the enemy being rather fond of sending gas shells into the area.

At times heavy shells dropped on the ground above, and as the shock was apt to dislodge portions of the roof, some parts were rendered unsafe. Most of the dangerous parts were propped or barricaded off, but several slight casualties were caused by falls of chalk. Cooking presented a serious problem, owing to the smoke from the fires, and water was difficult to obtain. The Divisional Band used to come and give concerts, and when they were playing in one of the large caves lit up by electric light the effect was like a scene in a pantomime. The men were not permitted to go up on to the top during daylight, as the entrances were under observation from German balloons, and life in the potted air was rather trying, the fine dust and damp affecting the throat.

The Division took over the front on the forward slope of Telegraph Hill and in front of Tilloy, and was now under the XVII. Corps. The situation and intention of the enemy on this Sector was still uncertain, and Battle positions were reconnoitred for the Battalion, in case of attack, and Lewis gun posts were selected in the Blangy reserve trenches, the Battalion standing to arms daily at 5 a.m., a procedure which much interfered with the men's rest after working all night, but as soon as the situation had cleared the standing to was cancelled. The line held by the Division consisted of a series of posts with support and reserve lines in rear, but, as the enemy had advanced in this Sector in March, the defences were rather undefined and work was concentrated on getting them into order. No day work was possible in front of the Beaurains Ridge, as the whole of it was under observation from Monchy. On April 9th Dainville was heavily shelled, and the Battalion's transport being forced to evacuate their quarters, moved to Wagonlieu, and later to Wanquetin. On the 11th the enemy attacked the posts on the Divisional front, and at 9-30 a.m. the alarm was sounded and the Battalion stood to arms. The attack, however, failed to develop, and by mid-day the situation was clear again. A great amount of wiring was done by the Battalion, the whole of the intermediate line being protected by April 16th, with two complete belts of double apron fence. Blangy fire and Blangy support trenches, which ran across the whole of the Divisional front, were made continuous and repaired.

On April 23rd the Division extended its front northwards by taking over a piece of line from the 15th Division up to the railway. In order to join up with the trenches on the north side of the railway, the Division decided to construct an entirely new support line to the Feuchy Switch, with communication trenches joining up to Feuchy fire trench, this work being entrusted solely to the Cheshires. The first work to be done was to put out two rows of double apron fence. This was completed in one night, some 2,000 yards of wire fence being erected. This was a very creditable performance, only possible owing to the men's wiring skill, and to the organization of the working parties and formation of dumps of material at suitable points.

Aeroplane Photograph of Feuchy Trenches.

Aeroplane Photograph of Arras shewing Battalion Head Quarters.

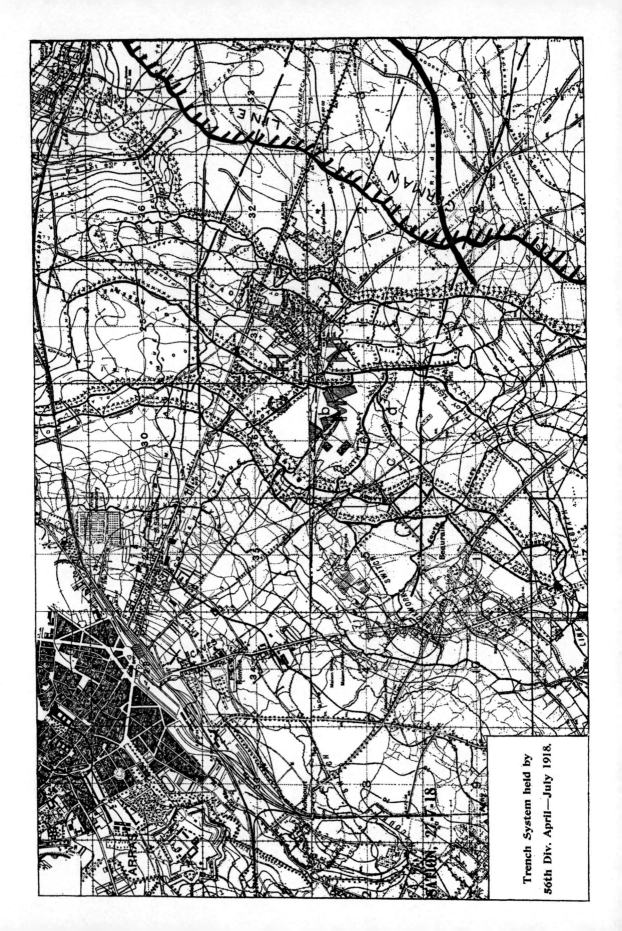

Trench System held by 56th Div. April—July 1918.

On May 8th the Battalion moved from the Ronville Caves to billets in Rue de Capucines, Arras. The billets taken over, although damaged, were very good, being large houses, and in several of them plenty of furniture was to be found. The furnished houses seemed to be a great source of anxiety to the town major, and the zealousness of his billet wardens led to more than one amusing contretemps. All the houses occupied had cellars, which were fitted up for occupation with bunks, and an elaborate system of gas curtains was installed, gas shelling being an ever present danger. Each group of billets had gas and aeroplane sentries, on duty by day and night, who gave the alarm by means of rattles and gongs.

The comfort of the men in these new quarters was much greater than in the Caves, and a regular service of baths was always available at the Schramm Barracks, where clean underclothing could be obtained and the uniforms cleansed by means of the " Thresh Disinfestator." There were several small shops open in the town which, however, were " out of bounds," but this disadvantage was counteracted by the supplies available at the Regimental Canteen and that of the Y.M.C.A. in the Petit Place.

During May work was concentrated on the new Feuchy system, which was completed by the middle of the month. A new fire trench, some 1,200 yards long, called North Alley Switch, was also dug, and repairs carried out to Scottish Avenue, North Alley and the Blangy Line, all communication trenches being fire stepped and wired on either side. During June, South Alley was extended and fire bayed, and a large amount of work put in on a new trench, Tilloy Reserve, which was required owing to an alteration of the system of holding the line in case of a heavy attack. During this month each of the Companies moved back in turn to Dainville for a week's rest and Infantry training. Certain experiments were carried out by the authorities during this month, one of these being the growing of mustard seed on the parapets of newly-dug trenches for the purpose of camouflage. The experiment was quite futile, as when the seed came up it rapidly grew to a foot in height, obscuring the view of anyone on the firestep, and as it flowered yellow it rather indicated than concealed the position of the trench. In addition to spasmodic shelling, Arras naturally received attention from hostile aeroplanes; one bomb dropped just in front of one of the billets, but did no harm to the occupants, although it considerably damaged the building, and blew off all the leaves from the trees in the vicinity of where it dropped. On another occasion at night an enemy aeroplane flew low over the billeting area, dropping "Verey" lights and firing a machine gun.

On July 13th the Battalion was relieved by the Canadian Pioneers, and marched to Hauteville, on the 14th to Gouy, on the 15th to Averdoignt, and on the 18th to Estree Cauchy, where Infantry training was intensively carried out. During the Battalion's stay in this village, the enemy's night flying bombing planes were very active raiding the back areas and railheads. On one occasion bombs were dropped in the village, one of these being in dangerous proximity to one of the billets.

Lieut.-Colonel A. C. Crookenden, D.S.O., who had been the Brigade Major during our training at Northampton, paid us a visit here, he then being G.S.O. 1 of the 11th Division, which was in the area just north of Estree Cauchy.

On July 28th some very successful Battalion sports were held, "A" Company winning the championship. A feature of the sports was a series of three races for the children of the village, which caused great enthusiasm amongst the parents and proved immensely popular. The following letter of thanks was subsequently sent to the Commanding Officer by the Maire :—

Departement du Pas-de-Calais, Mairie d'Estree-Cauchy.
Arrondissement de Bethune,
Canton D'Houdain.

Mon Colonel,

Je soussigné Brayelle Darius, Maire de la Commune d'Estree-Cauchy ai l'honneur de vous presenter mes plus chaleureus remerciments pour les divertissements que vous avez procurés a la populations civil le dimanche 28 Courant.

Nous avons admiré vos jeux sportifs et avons éprouvé un réel plaisir a voir vos hommes, officers et soldats, confondus dans un reélle camaraderie respectueuse, sentiment qui fait l'harmonie et la force d'une armeé.

Les enfants qui ont pris part a vos jeux ont été enchantés des prix que vous avez decernés aux vainqueurs.

Pour eux je vous dis égalment Merci.

Je vous prie de recevoir, Mon Colonel, l'assurance de mes sentiments les meilleurs.

Le Maire,
D. BRAYELLE,
Estree-Cauchy, le 30 Juillet, 1918.

On August 1st the Battalion left Estree Cauchy and moved to its old quarters in Arras, the long march being broken at Mont St. Eloi, where teas and a rest were taken. Their stay in Arras only lasted a fortnight, the Divisional front being further to the south than on their previous tour of duty, and the work was mainly in repair of trenches and wiring.

The Divisional competition for cross-country running for the Gropi cup was held on August 15th at Dainville. The cup was presented to the Division by Lieut.-Colonel J. E. G. Groves, C.M.G., T.D. The race was a team race of sixteen runners from each unit, and was held under ideal weather conditions. Fifteen teams entered, and the result was a win for the team of the 1st London Royal Fusiliers (T.F.), the Divisional Machine Gun Battalion's team being second, and that of the 1/5th Cheshire Regiment third.

On the 16th the Battalion was relieved by the 9th Bn. Gordon Highlanders (Pioneers), and moved to Beaufort by light railway. Whilst there, orders were received that all stores and kits were to be cut down to a minimum in view of offensive operations and an advance, and on the 21st the Division was transferred to the VI. Corps, taking over the Croisilles Front. The Battalion marched the same night to La Bazique, the column only just avoiding a bombing raid *en route*, which unfortunately caught a few of the billeting party who had gone on in front.

On the 22nd orders were received that 168 Brigade would attack the following morning, and " B " and " C " Companies were placed at the disposal of the Brigade and moved up to Blairville, accompanied by " A " echelon of the transport. On the 23rd the Division captured Boiry and Boyelles, and Head Quarters and " A " Company moved up to Blairville to bivouac in trenches. On the 24th the Division captured Summit Trench, and all three Companies moved forward to trenches south of Boisleux au Mont. " A " Company was specially employed with an R.E. Company in sinking wells in the bed of the Cojeul River, the water supply in this region causing considerable anxiety to the Authorities. Head Quarters followed to the same area the following day, bivouacking in a sunken road. The advance of the Division on this Sector of the front was handicapped by the lack of roads and the bad condition of those that did exist, and a great amount of work was thrown on to the Battalion in getting these forward roads and tracks fit for guns and transport. Luckily the weather was fine and dry. In this work they were greatly assisted by the discovery of a large supply of road material at a dump, at the Station at Boyelles, which the enemy had abandoned and left undamaged. On the 28th the Division captured Croisilles, and on the 31st Bullecourt, overcoming some stiff opposition, especially at the latter village. The same day the Division was relieved by the 52nd Division, the Battalion's work being taken over by the 19th Northumberland Fusiliers. " A " and " B " Companies then commenced work under the C.E. Corps on communications, and " C " Company was engaged, under the Divisional burial officer, in clearing the battlefield round Bullecourt, being relieved after a few days by " B " Company, which in turn was relieved by " A " Company.

On September 4th, Head Quarters moved up east of Croisilles. On arrival at their destination and whilst commencing to erect their bivouacs they were shelled by high velocity shells at a long range. One of these landed close to the constructing party, causing considerable casualties, two being killed and nineteen wounded. Amongst the latter were the Adjutant Captain Rowlands, the Medical Officer, Lieut. Miller, and Regimental Sergeant-Major J. Wilcock, all the R.A.M.C. Staff, and all except one of the Battalion's pioneers. On September 7th the Division was transferred to the XXII. Corps and took over the Sector Recourt-Eterpigny. Battalion Head Quarters moved to Les Fosses Farm, on the Arras-Cambrai road, and the Companies to trenches south-east of Monchy. " B " Company was placed at the disposal of the Corps for light railway work and moved to bivouacs near Pont de Jour. " A " and " C " Companies were employed in making new artillery tracks and repairing and bridging the existing ones leading up to Vis en Artois, and constructing machine gun emplacements for the Divisional Machine Gun Battalion. On the 24th orders were received that the 11th and 56th Divisions would follow behind the Canadians crossing the Canal du Nord at Marquion and then, by swinging to the north, form a protective flank to the Canadian Corps along the River Sensee. The orders to the Battalion were that they would be employed in making the crossings of the canal with the Royal Engineers on zero day. Battalion Head Quarters accordingly moved up to Dury Cross Roads and the Companies further forward. On the 26th a change in the hour of zero necessitated a complete alteration of operation orders, by Major Ellington, M.C., who was in command during the Commanding

Officer's absence on leave. All three Companies, with Lewis guns, were allotted their respective rendezvous, transport arrangements were made for carting bridging material, and everything was ready for the attack the following morning, all details had been minutely worked out with the greatest care and foresight, and to this was due to a considerable extent the subsequent success of the Battalion's operations. On the following morning, the 27th, the great attack took place, the Canadians crossing the canal and brushing aside all opposition and going straight ahead at a great pace, leaving the mopping up to the 56th Division. Battalion Head Quarters established its forward report centre at 9 a.m., and at 10-15 a.m. " A " Company received orders to move to the east of Baralle. They encountered artillery and machine gun fire, but passed through the leading infantry of the Division, who were moving by sectional rushes, and reached the east side of the village. A strong patrol was then sent out with Lewis guns, as parties of the enemy were still holding the west bank of the Canal and had not by that time been dispersed. Lewis gun fire was opened, and owing to the bold and clever handling of the patrol the enemy was driven off, a bag of nineteen prisoners being captured. For this exploit Lieut. G. H. Williams was awarded the Military Cross and Sergt. Cruickshank the Military Medal. By 12 noon the situation on the Canal was reported clear, and within the space of an hour all the bridging material was carried down and dumped. By 1 p.m. the situation on the Agache river (to the east of the Canal) was clear and material carried forward for bridging. A track was flagged from Baralle to Marquion, and by 2-15 p.m. 512 Field Company, with " A " Company, had got a bridge across the canal. " B " Company with 513 Field Company constructed a fascine track and assisted in the construction of another bridge, and " C " Company was employed in cutting ramps through the steep banks of the canal to a third pontoon bridge which had been thrown across.

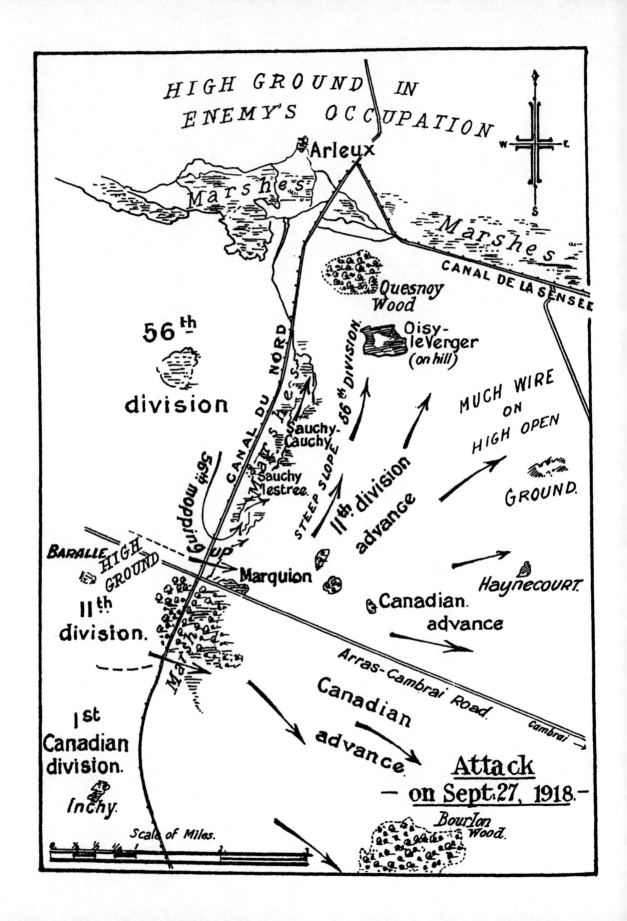

On the following two days the Battalion was employed working in shifts day and night on the various bridges and their approaches. The attack was one of the prettiest combined manœuvres imaginable, which completely outwitted the enemy. In place of a general attack on the whole front (which besides the canal and strong fortifications was a low marshy strip 500 to 800 yards wide, with big fields of wire), the Canadians crossed south of the main Arras—Cambrai road and spread out. The 11th Division crossed behind them and turning northwards took over the northern part of the ground. After the 11th the 56th came over about the same place, and went up between the 11th and the Canal. The fighting in this important corner was very severe, especially round the Bois de Quesnoy, but the advance went on, the Divisions capturing Sauchy Cauchy, Oisy le Verger, and Epinoy, and finally establishing themselves on the Canal de la Sensee. On October 1st " A " Company was billeted at Baralle, and " B " Company moved to Sauchy Cauchy. Both of these villages received considerable attention from the enemy's guns, and on October 3rd " A " Company's Head Quarters received a direct hit from a high velocity shell, which wrecked the house. By a perfect miracle all the occupants of the house escaped with a severe shaking, except Captain H. L. Churton, who was severely wounded. Owing to the frequent shelling of Baralle, " A " Company was withdrawn from the village and moved back to the old quarters occupied previously by " B " Company. On October 9th and 10th the Division took over the front held by the 11th Division, and on the 11th was transferred from the XXII. Corps to the Canadian Corps. Considerable fighting took place round Arleux, and Aubigny le Bac on the north side of the Sensee, the Companies being employed partly on work under the Brigades and partly in improving communications.

It became evident at this period that the enemy contemplated a retirement, as nightly the glare from burning villages and towns could be seen in their lines, that of Douai especially being noticeable. On the 14th orders were received that the Division would be relieved by the 4th Canadian Division, and on the 15th the Battalion, on relief by the 10th Canadian Engineers, marched to Marquion, now a railhead, and entrained at midnight for Agnez-lez-Duisans, arriving there the following morning at ten and proceeding to huts and billets at Maroeuil, which were very conveniently arranged, containing a set of hot baths and a large hut which was utilised as a canteen and recreation room, and for lectures. During the Battalion's stay here a slight epidemic of influenza broke out. On October 31st the Division was again transferred to the XXII. Corps and ordered to move by motor lorries to the Lieu St. Amand and Douchy area. The Battalion embussed at 9 a.m., and after a most interesting run, through the battle fields and through Cambrai, reached Neuville sur l'Escaut about 5 p.m. This was a village inhabited by the French who had been under German rule, and they presented a pitiable sight, being half starved and very down-trodden in appearance. They greatly appreciated the different treatment which they received from our troops, who shewed the greatest kindness to them. The whole country had been terribly devastated by the enemy, railways, bridges, culverts and roads having been destroyed so as to delay our advance. On November 2nd the Division relieved the 49th Division in the Saultain Sector, and from that date until the Armistice the enemy was being continually pressed back, covering his retreat with strong rear guards. On the 2nd the Battalion moved to Pyramid de Denain, relieving the 19th Bn. Lancashire Fusiliers. On November 3rd the enemy retired and the Division pushed ahead. In view of the speed of the advance and in order to lighten the transport and the load to be carried by the men, all blankets and packs were dumped at Pyramid de Denain and left under a small guard.

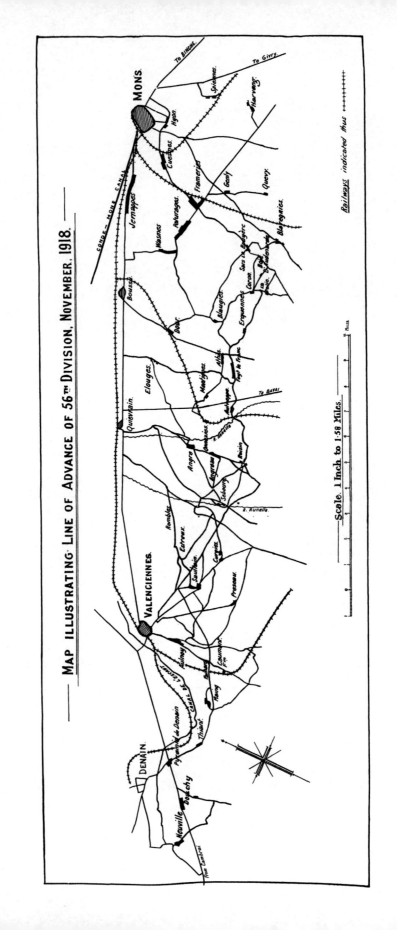

The same day " B " Company went forward to Saultain. On the morning of the 4th, Battalion Head Quarters moved to Caumont Farm, but owing to the pace of the advance, moved again in the afternoon to Saultain. Whilst at Caumont Farm the transport was shelled by long range guns, which caused several casualties to the horses, a serious loss at that stage.

On the 4th the Division captured Sebourg, and on the 5th Angreau. " C " Company moved forward to Sebourquiaux, and "A" Company joined the 169th Brigade for work, "B" Company being retained at Saultain to complete the filling in of the craters in the roads there. On November 6th the advance was slightly checked on a strong position on the River Honelle, but after a stiff action the opposition was driven back and Angre captured. On the 7th and 8th the advance was continued to Harveng. The three Divisions in the Corps had been advancing on parallel lines, but a change in tactics was now adopted, whereby the 63rd (Naval) Division moved forward as an advance guard, covering the whole of the Corps front.

On the 7th, Head Quarters moved to Sebourg, " A " and " B " Companies pushing on to Autreppe on the 8th, where Head Quarters and " C " Company joined them the following day. Owing to the speed of the advance and the lack of roads on the Divisional front, and owing to the number of craters blown in the roads by the enemy in their retreat, the state of the communications of the Division became a very serious matter, and the whole of the energies of the Battalion were concentrated in getting them fit for horse transport and lorries. The crossing of the Rhonelle was a very difficult problem. At this point the only road in the Divisional area was blocked by the demolition of a viaduct, over the stream and the road which ran alongside it ; only one light trestle bridge could be erected, to get horse transport across the river, and in addition the rain had converted the roads into a sea of mud. The Battalion gained great credit at this spot for the speed with which they cleared a passage through the débris of the viaduct. On November 10th, " A " Company moved on to La Folie, " B " to Coron, and Head Quarters and " C " to Athis, the craters in rear having all been made passable, and other innumerable craters further forward were worked on. On November 11th a telegram was received from XXII. Corps : " Hostilities will cease at 11 hours November 11th, and troops will stand fast on line reached at that hour, which will be reported to Corps. Defensive precautions will be maintained, and there will be no intercourse of any description with the enemy." The Armistice was received by all with great relief, but no demonstrations or excitement were noticeable. It was undoubtedly a great relaxation to be free from the strain at night of hearing an enemy bombing plane coming over and wondering if he was going to drop bombs on your billets, and also to be able to move about freely, without listening for the scream of approaching shells. There was, however, no cessation of the Battalion's work, as the question of road repair and reconstruction was of vital importance to enable supplies to be got forward to the most advanced troops, the railways being all out of action for miles to the rear. The chief work was on the series of five craters near the Bois d'Audenarde and craters in the villages of Sars-le-Bruyere and Blaregnies, " C " Company moving up to Le Rambourg to be near the site of their work. Great care had to be exercised in the repair of roads, which the enemy had mined, and also to avoid the various booby traps he had laid. The craters blown by the enemy had been very systematically planned, and in the majority of cases were at cross roads, all four roads thus being impassable, or where the road ran on an embankment ; their depth varied from ten to twenty feet.

The following special orders of the day were published in Battalion orders :—

(a) Special Order of the Day by Marshal Foch,
   Commander-in-Chief of the Allied Armies. 12/11/1918.

Officers, Non-Commissioned Officers, and Soldiers of the Allied Armies.

After bringing the enemy's attack to a stand by your stubborn defence, you attacked him without respite for several months, with inexhaustible energy and unwavering faith.

You have won the greatest battle in history and have saved the most sacred of all causes, the Liberty of the world.

Well may you be proud.

You have covered your standards with immortal glory, and the gratitude of posterity will ever be yours.

(Signed) F. FOCH, Marshal of France,
   Commander-in-Chief of the Allied Armies.

(b) Special Order of the Day by Field-Marshal Sir Douglas Haig,
   K.T., G.C.B., G.C.V.O., K.C.I.E., Commander-in Chief,
   British Armies in France. 13/11/1918.

After more than four years of war, the enemy has been forced to ask for an armistice and has accepted the terms dictated by the Allies. Hostilities have been suspended and we may look forward to the early conclusion of a just and honourable peace.

At the moment of the definite triumph of those principles of liberty and right for which we entered the war, I desire to thank all ranks of all services of the British Armies under my command for the noble share they have taken in bringing about this great and glorious result.

My thanks are due to the Officers, Non-Commissioned Officers and Men of the Fighting Forces (including the R.A.F.) who have served under my command in the prolonged struggle which has worn down and broken the strength of our opponents. Winter and summer the fierce strain has never ceased, has never for a moment been relaxed. Long and trying periods of trench fighting, countless raids and minor operations have bridged the gaps between the great battles on the Somme, at Arras, Messines, Ypres, Cambrai, and finally the tremendous conflicts of the present year, now crowned by victory.

In action you have been magnificent, equal to all changes of fortune, facing all dangers and surmounting all difficulties, your gallantry never failing, your courage most resolute, your devotion to duty unquestioning. Out of action, your time has been devoted, with a cheerfulness and energy undiminished by dangers and hardships undergone, to constant training and to the effort to make yourselves still more efficient. On such occasions your consistent good conduct and soldier-like behaviour have won for the British Army the esteem and lasting goodwill of the Allied peoples amongst whom you have lived.

To the non-combatant and auxiliary services, including the many thousands of women who by devoted work in so many capacities have assisted in the victory of our arms, I desire to express my deep gratitude for the essential service you have rendered.

No General has been given more loyal and whole-hearted support by all ranks of the Commanders, Staffs, Departments and Services under him. No General ever yet commanded an Army of which he had greater reason to be proud.

By your efforts and those of the gallant Armies of our Allies, the nations of the world have been saved from a great danger. You have fought for the sanctity of your homes and for the liberties of those who will come after you. Generations of free peoples, both of your own race and of all countries, will thank you for what you have done.

We do not forget those who have fallen, and by their sacrifice have made our triumph possible. The memory of those who fought in the early battles of the war, few indeed in number but unconquerable in spirit, and the thought of all the brave men who have since died, live in our hearts to-day.

Our task is not yet finished, though the end is in sight. Until such time as the terms of armistice have been complied with and the conclusion of peace allows us to return once more to our homes, I rely confidently upon you to maintain on all occasions the same high standard of discipline, efficiency and good conduct which has always distinguished the British Army.

(Signed) D. HAIG, F.M.,
Commander-in-Chief,
British Armies in France.

CHAPTER VI.

After the Armistice : Demobilization.

RETURN OF CADRE TO ENGLAND.

SHORTLY after the Armistice orders were received that the Battalion would proceed with the Division into Germany, and immediate preparations were made for cleaning and smartening everything up, but after an interval this order was countermanded. On November 15th a party of three Officers and 100 other ranks, under Captain A. H. Jolliffe, M.C., embussed and travelled to Mons to form part of the 56th Divisional Detachment, under Brigadier-General Coke, at the official entry into the Town of the 1st Army, under General Sir H. S. Horne, K.C.B., K.C.M.G. The troops marched past the General, who took the salute at the Hotel de Ville, in the Grand Place, surrounded by the leading citizens of the town; the streets and squares, gay with flags, were packed with people, who gave their deliverers a most enthusiastic reception.

The following is a special order by General Sir H. S. Horne, K.C.B., K.C.M.G., Commanding First Army :—

15/11/1918.

I desire to place upon record my appreciation of the general bearing of the troops of the First Army which took part in the parade at Mons to-day.

The smart turn out, steadiness on parade, good marching and soldier-like appearance produced a lasting impression upon those who witnessed the ceremonial. That such was possible after four years of continuous warfare is the highest tribute to the splendid spirit which has animated the troops of the British Empire and which has led on to the victory achieved.

(Signed) H. S. HORNE, General,
Commanding First Army.

In the last week in November the Division moved into the Mons area, and on November 28th the Battalion marched to Spiennes, an agricultural village south-east of Mons, which had been the right of the line held by the British at the Battle of Mons in 1914. This village, which was only just large enough to accommodate the Battalion, one Company of which, "A," was billeted at the adjoining hamlet of Malplaquet, afforded every facility for recreation, and three excellent football grounds were obtained. When the Division had settled down, a comprehensive educational scheme was set in motion, and was taken advantage of by the men with commendable keenness. During December the Battalion was employed in clearing away the débris of a viaduct over three streams close to the village, the block made by the demolitions having caused extensive floods. This work was continued until January, when it was taken over by the Belgian authorities. Football and sports were indulged in and every possible opportunity for recreation given to the men. Towards the middle of the month the demobilization scheme was promulgated, and on the 11th the first men were sent home. On Christmas Day a very successful series of dinners were held, the Division having arranged to procure turkeys from Paris, whilst some excellent Belgian beer was procured from Mons. This town being only an hour's walk from the village, was naturally a great attraction, and its shops did a roaring trade with the British troops at profiteering prices. There were two theatres in the town, which gave opera performances twice a week, and several Cinema Halls, and the "Bow Bells," the Divisional concert party, produced an excellent pantomime and played to packed houses nightly. A number of race meetings were held on the racecourse, arranged by the Corps and the different Divisions in the neighbourhood, and motor lorry excursions to these were freely patronised, as were other trips which were

Railway Viaduct at Spiennes   (Blown up by the Germans.)

Clearing debris of demolished Viaduct from Stream at Spiennes, December, 1918.

1918.   1916.
56th Division Association Football Cups won by the Battalion.

Battalion Football XI.
Winners of the 56th Division Football Association Cup, 1918.

arranged to places of interest in the neighbourhood. An inter-Platoon Football Competition was organized in the Battalion, and created some keen competition; some excellent material for the Battalion's team, which was continually being affected by the loss of men sent away for demobilization, was discovered by this means. In January the Divisional Association Football Competition started, and the Battalion's XI. again won the cup after a series of close and exciting matches. They defeated in the first round Divisional Head Quarters, in the second round the 3rd London Royal Fusiliers, in the third the 282nd Brigade Royal Field Artillery, after a very close game, and in the semi-final the 2/3rd London Field Ambulance. The final was played before a large gate, the Divisional Commander and his Staff being present, the Battalion's opponents being the 280th Brigade Royal Field Artillery, and after a game full of excitement no goals were scored. On the game being replayed the Cheshires won after having much the best of the game by two goals to nil. The team was :—Goal, Corpl. J. King; backs, Sergt. F. Kay, Corpl. W. Yearsley; half-backs, Pte. C. H. Todd, Sergt. J. Moss, Pte. A. Furness; forwards, Pte. P. Wright, Pte. J. Wood, Lance-Corpl. R. Dewsnap, Pte. F. Dodson, Pte. J. E. Wynne. Only three of this team were members of the victorious XI. of 1916-17.

The numbers of men sent home for demobilization gradually increased and by the end of January the strength of the Battalion was only just over 500. During February and March large parties were sent to England, and, on March 1st, a detachment of six Officers and one hundred and four other ranks, retainable men, were drafted to the 7th Battalion Cheshire Regiment, on the Rhine.

On March 20th the Battalion moved to Jemappes on the west of Mons. Here it remained until it was diminished to its cadre strength of three Officers and thirty-six other ranks, with stores and transport but no horses, all these having been called in. The necessary animals required were furnished from a pool, formed in the Division, from which they were obtained as occasion arose. Whilst in this town, which was a mining one of the usual type, with cobbled streets, time passed rather wearily; stores were checked and made correct and it was a question of waiting for orders to proceed to England. At the beginning of April expectations of an early move were officially raised, but nothing came of them, and it was not until the middle of May that the Division received any orders to move.

Finally the Cadre left Jemappes on June 9th, moving by train to Antwerp, where it rested one night, and the following day its transport was loaded on Barge P.D. 3, the personnel embarking on the transport Sicilian at 2 p.m. After a perfect passage down the Scheldt and across the North Sea, Tilbury was reached at 10 a.m. The cadre disembarked at 1 p.m., and leaving Tilbury by train at 2-30 p.m., they reached Fenchurch Street and marched to Aldgate, where the tube was taken to Gower Street. The cadre was billeted for the night at the Y.M.C.A. Hut at Euston, and on the 13th they left Euston, reaching Chester at 4 p.m. Their reception at Chester is described in the Chester *Courant* of June 18th as follows :—

> "The Cadre of the 5th Battalion of the Cheshire Regiment, the Earl of Chester's and the City of Chester's own, had their homecoming on Friday afternoon. Like many long expected things, it came very suddenly in the end, for news as to the date of their arrival was very indefinite till the morning, which brought a message like a bolt from the blue. Hurried preparations were made, the news was circulated as well as possible, and the City threw on its bunting garb, which had been lying ready for weeks. The weather was just as obliging, for up to nearly three o'clock, when the train that brought the Cadre was expected, the overcast skies and the winds had more than a suspicion of heavy rain about them. But the sun lit through the dulness, and the Cadre of the Unit in which the City is most interested, and with which it has the closest personal ties, marched out of the station into a Chester that was good to look upon, a place not gloomy, but sun-flooded, and brave with the colours of flags and banners that were hung out in welcome.

Valenciennes Railway Station. (Destroyed by the Germans.)

Loading 60-pounder Guns on H.M. Transport "Sicilian" at Antwerp.

The Cadre of the 1/5th (E. of C.) Cheshire Regiment embarking on H.M. Transport "Sicilian" at Antwerp, June 11th, 1919.

Loading the Battalion's Transport on Barge P.D. 3 at Antwerp.

RETURN OF CADRE TO ENGLAND.

The Cadre which is composed of 36 Warrant Officers, N.C.O.'s and Men, was under the command of Lieut. Colonel W. A. V. Churton, a son of Chester, needless to say, and one whose connection with the Battalion, and especially the City Company, goes far enough back for him to have the letters T.D. after his name. His war service was recognised and rewarded with the D.S.O. The other Officers with the C.O., were Capt. G. Fell Milner and Capt. and Quartermaster W. C. Cunningham. The returning soldiers were officially received and welcomed at the station by Colonel Thompson, C.B., Secretary of the Cheshire Territorial Force Association, and Capt. E. D. Dickson, T.D. A party of Officers and Men who had served Overseas with the Battalion also attended to give the home-comers that very best welcome, which comes from old comrades in arms. Among other Officers on the arrival platform were Lieut. Col. A. G. Hamilton, O.B.E., R.A.M.C., Majors Ashton, M.C., T.D., N. B. Ellington, M.C., Timmins and A. J. Musgrave; Captains H. L. Churton, Oscar Johnson, H. N. Hignett, A. H. Cowap, and R. W. Miller; Lieutenants Frater, Spicer, Wyman, Arthur Birch and Armstrong, Sergt. Major Mellor, O.B.E., Chief Clerk Territorial Force Association, was with the band of Old Comrades. On leaving the train the Cadre were relieved of, or to use the military expression, 'dumped' their marching order equipment, leaving it in charge of a fatigue party that had been thoughtfully provided from the Depôt at the Castle, and another very praiseworthy item of the reception programme was the supply of beer, and for those who did not fancy it, the gas and bubbling of exhilerating 'pop.' The Old Comrades party, it should be mentioned, were under the command of Colonel T. J. Smith, V.D.

The train was very late, which was a blessing in disguise, as it led to a thickening of the crowds that lined the streets and the rows. Consequently, the men were met with a fine reception as they marched through the streets to the Town Hall Square, where the Mayor (Sir John Frost) was waiting to receive them, and to hand them back their Colours. Speeches were made and the Cadre was told how glad the City was to see the nucleus of its own Battalion again, and after being being invited to supper at the Bars Hotel in the evening, all that was left of the 5th gave ringing cheers, and went their way to their old Drill Hall.

The Town Hall Square was crowded, and a special Guard from the Castle Depôt was on parade, under the command of Capt. Matterson and Lieut. A. Squires, M.C. Major Jackson had charge of the arrangements, and Majors Clarke, D.S.O., and N. R. Freeman, M.C., also attended.

The London train conveying the Cadre drew into the station at 3-38, nearly an hour late. The men having deposited their kits on the platform proceeded to a waiting room for refreshment, and re-appeared on the platform wearing oak leaves in their caps. They were formed up, and having fixed bayonets, Lieut.-Col. Vere Churton gave the command

'Quick March,' the Cadre at once moving off into the street where there was an assembled crowd to greet them. Headed by the Band of the 3rd V.B. Cheshire Regiment, a number of the members of which had been mustered by Bandmaster Geo. Stratford and Staff Sergt. Morris, the Cadre marched to the Town Hall Square. The streets were lined with people all the way. In Eastgate Street and at the Cross, and again in the Town Hall Square they were particularly thick. Much enthusiasm prevailed. As the Cadre marched up Northgate Street into the Town Hall Square and came to a halt below the steps, one could not help being impressed with their soldierly appearance. Well built, their faces tanned a deep brown, carrying themselves with easy confidence, and doing their drill with the nonchalant efficiency which distinguishes the overseas veteran from his often mechanically perfect brother of the English parade ground, they were well worth studying. They looked harder than nails and fitter than fiddles, and quite worthy to represent the unit whose field work had been advertised as a model for the Army by G.H.Q. Lieut.-Colonel Churton, for whom it must have been a very proud moment, went up the steps and received a warm personal welcome from the Mayor and Sheriff, standing near whom were the Mayoress (Lady Frost), the Town Clerk (Mr. J. H. Dickson), several members of the Aldermanic Bench, Colonel Thompson, Colonel Kellie, Mr. E. Peter Jones, etc. Col. Churton was heard to explain that the Cadre's late arrival was due to engine trouble. The speeches followed immediately.

The Mayor, in extending a welcome to the officers and men of the Cadre, told them how the unexpectedness of their arrival had had its effect on the public attendance but that Chester received them, all the same, with the heartiest congratulations and thanks. After referring to the deep impression they made on the King, who reviewed them at Cambridge shortly before they went to France under the command of Colonel Groves, early in 1915, Sir John spoke of the Battalion's work at Hill 60 and Gommecourt, where, he declared, they won undying praise. From that time until the Armistice they had given every satisfaction, and won great honour, and the citizens had the pleasure that day of welcoming them home again with feelings of gratitude for the glorious part they had played during the last four and a half years in maintaining the traditions of the regiment. 'It is now well known,' Sir John exclaimed, 'that the Territorial Force was the salvation of the Country in her hour of sore distress.' 'The citizens of Chester have all through the War recognised,' he went on, 'that you are the Battalion of the Regiment most closely connected with the City. They have followed your movements with the greatest of interest and pride, and throughout coming generations your performances will be held up to those who follow in your footsteps as a pattern of patriotic self-sacrifice for King and Country. I am only echoing the wish of all the citizens when I express to you the hope that you will resume your civil occupations and that you will spend many happy years of peace and prosperity in your native City and Country.'

The Sheriff spoke with the brevity and good-heartedness that characterise him. He mentioned that he joined the Volunteers' predecessors of the 5th Battalion in 1880. The few words he uttered were of pride in the Battalion, in the Cadre of which, he said, was his nephew (Sergt. Tom Burkhill) who had 'been through it all for four and a half years.'

Colonel Thompson, C.B., in his official capacity, and at the express request of the Territorial Force, told the Cadre of the pride the Association had had in following the work of the Battalion, and the pride it had in the welcome that the Mayor and Corporation had extended to them. The Mayor and the Corporation had done wonders for all Chester soldiers throughout the War. He wished to emphasise the great pride the Association had in the Battalion. When mobilized it numbered 950, exclusive of officers, during the next 17 months its numbers increased to 2,800 all voluntarily enlisted men, and the grand total was 6,800 men. That was the contribution of Chester and district to its infantry regiment. He said the Association was proud of them; it had every reason to be proud of them. They had heard from regular officers and regular commanders of the splendid name the 5th Cheshires had throughout the War for discipline. The other day it was reported to him that the Battalion's discipline was a by-word throughout the Division. Their work as pioneers had been commended by the very highest authorities, and he was personally told a fortnight ago that all the work that had to be done by the Pioneer Battalion of the 56th Division was safe to be done in a perfect manner and in due time. In conclusion, Colonel Thompson, addressing Colonel Churton and his men said: 'The Association can only express to you its great pride and thanks for all you have done.'

Lieut. Colonel Churton, D.S.O. in responding, said the Mayor had very rightly remarked that the Territorial Force, when it went out had the responsibility thrown upon it of upholding the great traditions of the Regular Battalions. They always bore that in mind, and he was confident that the example of the Regular Battalions of the Cheshire Regiment had been followed by the Junior Battalion with uncommonly satisfactory results. On behalf of all he represented, he would like to take the opportunity of offering hearty thanks for the reception and all the other good things they had received from the City. Various ladies and gentlemen had sent all sorts of comforts, which had been greatly appreciated by everybody concerned, and he now desired publicly to thank all those who had sent such things out. After a hint at, rather than a review of his Battalion's record, in the 5th and 56th Divisions, Colonel Churton said the 5th Division needed no comment from him, and that, if they wanted to know what the 56th Division did, let them read what Sir Douglas Haig said the day previous, and they would understand the sort of places they had been in, and the conditions they had worked under. He heartily thanked the Mayor, the Sheriff, and Colonel Thompson for their kind remarks.

The final stage of the Ceremony was short and impressive, The King's and the Regimental Colours, garlanded with oak leaves, were carried down the steps on to the Square, where the Mayor handed them to Captain Milner and Captain Hignett. In its way there was something solemn about Sir John's quotation of the words of Sir Charles Napier when presenting the Colours to the 1st Battalion on the 18th November, 1815. There is something perennial in the words, which run: 'Take your Colours, and let the ancient City of Chester, girt by its ancient, proud old Walls, exult in the glories of its own brave Regiment.' The Cadre with Colours flying then marched to the Drill Hall, where the Colours were deposited, and dismissed. In the evening the Mayor entertained the Cadre and a large number of Guests and ex-Members of the Battalion at the Bars Hotel, and after a memorable day the Cadre spent the night at the Castle. On the following day all the rank and file were sent to Prees Heath for demobilization, the officers being demobilized at the end of the month. Of the Cadre the following had gone out with the Battalion in February, 1915:—

    Lt.-Col. W. A. V. Churton, D.S.O., T.D.
    R.Q.M.S. T. Whitehead, M.S.M.
    C.Q.M.S. C. G. Hewitt, M.M.
    Sergt. F. Moss, M.S.M.
    Sergt. G. Cruickshank, M.M.
    Sergt. T. Burkhill.
    Sergt. W. Jackson.
    Lance-Corpl. T. Starkey.
    Lance-Corpl. F. Moran.
    Lance-Corpl. P. Loftus.
    Pte. C. Daniels.
    Pte. S. Oldfield.
    Pte. J. Beard.

On reaching Head Quarters the following telegram was sent to H.R.H. the Prince of Wales, who was at Princetown, Devon:—'5th Battalion, Cheshire Regiment, on return from active service abroad, salutes your Royal Highness, their Honorary Colonel. Lt.-Colonel Churton, Drill Hall, Chester.'

During the day the following reply was received from the Prince:— 'O.H.M.S. Buckingham Palace, Lt-Colonel Churton, Drill Hall, Chester. Prince of Wales desires me to thank you and all ranks of the 5th Battalion, Cheshire Regiment, for their very kind telegram.—Private Secretary.' "

The Mayor of Chester (Sir J. M. Frost) handing back the Battalion's Colours to the Cadre.

Reception of Cadre at Chester Town Hall.

CHAPTER VII.

Conclusion.

'The Earl of Chester came to me and shook me by the hand,
He said the Fifth Battalion was the finest in the land.
                                    Ta, Ra, Ra."

THESE, the first two lines of the Battalion's topical and marching song, composed at Northampton by Subalterns of the Battalion, and set to music by that versatile pianist the late 2nd Lieut. B. S. Walker, reflect the spirit and pride of the Regiment. The title " Earl of Chester's," originally conferred on the old 6th (Chester) Administrative Battalion of the Volunteers in 1870, and so inherited by the 5th Battalion, was the caution word on Battalion parades, and was an honour that was most zealously guarded by all ranks.

The discipline and *esprit de corps* of the Battalion was always of a high standard. This was due to the fact that all ranks realised that they had the great reputation of the regiment to uphold, and also that (with the exception of a draft of the Herefordshires, who proved themselves to be excellent soldiers) all reinforcements came to the Battalion from other Cheshire Battalions, and so felt that they had come amongst their friends and they had had the traditions of the regiment instilled into them. All reinforcements after landing in France proceeded to Rouen, which was the base depôt of the Battalion, and there they received a short course of instruction in trench warfare and (when the anti-gas equipment had been perfected) were put through the gas chamber to test their box respirators before being sent up to join their unit. In December 1917, a Pioneer

School was opened at Rouen, to which a Company Commander and three N.C.O's. from each Pioneer Battalion were sent for a course which lasted a month. This school was of great value, instruction being given in all the latest engineering methods, brought up-to-date in the light of war experience. In February a conference of Commanding Officers of Pioneer Battalions was held at the School, under the direction of the General Staff, when the organization and method of employment of Pioneer Battalions, and the suitability of their equipment, was fully discussed. As a result of this conference, the re-organization of Pioneer Battalions on a three Company basis was introduced, and a considerable reduction was made in the establishment of tools to be carried. When the great German offensive in March commenced, all those then attending the School were formed into an emergency battalion, which carried out a number of important works until the danger had passed; the Officers and men were then sent back to their units and the School was finally broken up.

In March 1918, orders were received that one hundred A.1 men had to be sent to the 10th Battalion Cheshire Regiment, and that their places would be filled by one hundred B.1 men. The B.1 men on arrival were all suffering from some complaint or weakness, and it is difficult to understand why the change was made (unless it was owing to lack of man power), as Pioneer work was of an exceptionally strenuous character, and these men proved a great source of anxiety. It was impossible to expect B.1 men to do the same amount of work as A.1 men, as they were not physically capable of doing it, through no fault of their own. It was also very hard on the Companies, who were unable to show full value for their work, owing to the presence of B.1 men in their ranks; this was especially marked in the case of digging trenches, all the men not being able to move the same amount of earth in a task. The B.1 men in several cases improved wonderfully, whilst several very soon went to hospital, but in spite of the fact that as many as possible were put on administrative or light work, it must be admitted that their presence in the Battalion very considerably affected the work, and on marches of any length they were always a source of trouble and anxiety, a large number of them being unable to carry their packs for any distance.

In one detail the Battalion always had a great reputation, namely, that of sanitation and cleanliness in billets; these most vital matters formed a very important part of their training at home, and the strictest attention to them was always paid during their service abroad. Billets were always improved at every place they visited, a matter of no difficulty, owing to the number of skilled tradesmen in the Battalion.

In addition to its work in the line, the Battalion was always being called upon by the Division to do work of every conceivable kind, from erecting a stage for the Divisional concert party, to reinterring a corpse which had been in a vault at Haplincourt for 100 years and had been dragged out by the Hun in search of plunder during his retreat ; or finding a man who was an expert at making soda water.

A large number of men were selected for commissions, and many of those who obtained them did remarkably well. Amongst the several Officers who became Staff Officers were Captain S. H. Smith, M.C., Staff Captain 53rd Infantry Brigade, and later D.A.A.G. XIII. Corps; Captain F. Bishop, M.C., Staff Captain 169th Infantry Brigade ; Captain T. L. C. Heald, M.C., G.S.O.3, 56th Division ; Captain A. J. Allmand, M.C., Chemical Adviser to 3rd Army ; Captain A. Burnett, Assistant Provost Marshal, Tank Corps.

The anniversaries of the Battalion's arrival in France were commemorated by an Officers dinner, these being the rare occasions when all the Officers messed together, as during the campaign company messes were the rule. The first of these was held in 1917 at Laventie, the second at the Officers' Club, Arras, and the last at the Officers' Club, Mons ; the only other occasions when a Battalion mess was held being during the Battalion's stay at Bray in December, 1915, and January, 1916, and a dinner at the Officers' Club at Bapaume in September, 1917.

During the Battalion's service in France no distinctive badges or marks (other than the Pioneer badges worn on the collar) were worn, except at the very end of the war, when the design of the interlaced " P " and Divisional Dagger was adopted for use on the front of the steel helmet, the colour being white. The Battalion's sign on its transport was the Divisional Dagger and " P," in white on a blue square.

The reason why the dagger was adopted as the Divisional sign, was because the dagger appears on the Arms of the City of London.

After the first German gas attack in April, 1915, the Battalion was supplied with a respirator consisting of a pad to be placed across the month ; this was soon succeeded by another pattern consisting of gauze and wadding, which whilst affording slight protection was not satisfactory or efficient. The next issue was a gas helmet made of flannel soaked in a chemical solution and fitted with eye pieces and an air valve ; this helmet was very hot and uncomfortable to wear. Later in the war, after a series of experiments, the box respirator was issued, which proved itself to be an absolute safeguard against gas and was not, after experience, such a disagreeable article to wear. The carrying of the box respirator in all advanced areas was compulsory, and in all front areas the respirator had to be worn in the alert position, ready to be put on at a moment's notice.

Cap Badge and Pioneer Collar Badges
worn by the Battalion.

Steel Helmet with 56th Divisional Sign.

Officers of "A" Company,
Dainville, 1918.

Lt. J F. Breeze.   2/Lt, A. C. Lisle.   2/Lt. A. Monk Jones.   2/Lt T R. Cook.
Lt. G. H. Williams, M.C.   Capt. O. Johnson, M.C.   Lt. R. Fell Milner.

"B" Company Officers, photographed in ruins of Ypres Cathedral,
April, 1915.

2/Lieut. T. L. C. Heald. Capt. W. A. V. Churton. Lieut. F. J. Bairstow.
Capt. H Caldecutt. 2/Lieut. N. Holmstrom.

Officers 1/5th (E. of C.) Cheshire Regiment.
Group taken at Spiennes, Belgium, December, 1918.

Lt. E. W. McEvoy.   Lt. H. R. Disley.   2/Lt. T. R. Cook.   2/Lt. A. Monk Jones.   Lt. A. C. Lisle.   Lt. J. L. Walker.   2/Lt. F. S. Church.   Lt. W. W. Arnold.
Lt. F. J. L. Roberts.   2/Lt. A. B. Smith.   Int. P. Guerin.   2/Lt. T. M. Anderson.   Qm. Lt. W. C. Cunningham.   Lt. J. E. Breeze.   Lt. K. N. Standish.   Lt. G. F. Milner.   Lt. G. T. Breach.   Lt. F. L. Moore.   Lt. F. E. Ashworth.
Rev. J. L. Sheppard.   Capt. H. W. Glendinning.   Lt. J. H. L. Gibson.   Capt. F. J. Bairstow.   2/Lt. G. C. Sandford.   Maj. N. B. Ellington, M.C.   Lt.-Col. W. A. V. Churton, D.S.O., T.D.
Capt. N. Armstrong, Adjt.   Capt. J. D. Salmon, M.C.   Capt. A. H. Jolliffe, M.C.   Lt. O. K. S. Laugharne.   Capt. G. R. Curl, M.O.R.C. (U.S.A.).

Honours and Awards.

C.M.G. - Lt.-Colonel J. E. G. Groves, T.D.

D.S.O. - Major (T/Lt.-Col.) W. A. V. Churton, T.D.

O.B.E. - Major H. Watts, T.D.
Major J. H. Davies
Capt. F. A. Freeth.

M.B.E. - Lieut. (Bt.-Major) C. Johnson.

MILITARY CROSS.

Capt. (A/Major) N. B. Ellington
„ L. Bengough
„ A. E. Hodgkin
„ O. Johnson
Lieut. (A/Capt.) T. L. C. Heald
„ „ F. Bishop.

Lieut. (A/Capt.) A. J. Allmand
„ „ S. H. Smith
„ „ A. H. Jolliffe
„ „ J. D. Salmon
„ G. H. Williams
„ G. McGowan.

French Croix de Guerre - Lieut. (A/Capt.) S. H. Smith, M.C.

Ordre du Merite Agricole - Lt.-Col. J. E. G. Groves, C.M.G., T.D.

MENTIONED IN DISPATCHES.

Lt.-Col. J. E. G. Groves, C.M.G., T.D. (3)
Major (T/Lt.-Col.) W. A. V. Churton, D.S.O., T.D. (3)
Major J. H. Davies, O.B.E.
Capt. (A/Major) N. B. Ellington, M.C.
„ L. Bengough, M.C.
„ A. Burnett (2)
, G. W. C. Hartley
„ H. L. Churton
„ T. L. C. Heald, M.C. (2)

Capt. H. N. Hignett (2)
Lieut. (A/Capt.) S. H. Smith, M.C. (3)
„ „ F. Bishop, M.C. (2)
„ „ A. J. Allmand, M.C.
„ „ E. S. Heron
„ E. W. Abraham
„ G. McGowan, M.C. (2)
„ C. J. Mead
„ J. H. L. Gibson
2nd Lieut. H. F. Davies.

o

HONOURS AND AWARDS.

DISTINGUISHED CONDUCT MEDAL.

1863	Sergeant	T. Lockley	1308	Private	L. Pollitt.
15605	Private	G. Cartwright			

MILITARY MEDAL.

1583	C.Q.M.S.	P. J. Fisher	15749	L/Corpl.	A. Beard
15602	Sergeant	S. Davies (& Bar)	1260	,,	F. Manton
3354	,,	L. Ratcliffe	240474	Sergeant	C. G. Hewitt
1687	,,	T. Price	240948	Private	J. Bellis
1262	C.S.M.	W. Cross	240588	,,	F. Morrison
1948	Sergeant	A. Graham	241164	,,	H. R. Mitchell
1419	,,	A. Lamb	240391	,,	S. Atherton
2137	,,	A. C. Gatcliffe	240606	Private	J. Royle
1531	L/Sergt.	H. Bramhall	241275	,,	C. Coombes
2329	Corporal	J. T. Stone	240958	,,	C. J. Doughty
1438	L/Corpl.	F. W. Dutton	240477	Sergeant	G. Cruickshank
2013	Private	G. Dearn	240211	L/Corpl.	G. A. Passey
2277	,,	G. Maunder	240231	Private	S. Bramhall
2344	,,	W. Murphy	240072	Sergeant	W. Skillicorn
2310	,,	W. G. Stolte	240124	,,	G. H. Ogden
2015	,,	F. Griffiths	240874	Private	J. Price.
5748	,,	J. Holland			

MERITORIOUS SERVICE MEDAL.

5587	R.S.M.	J. F. Wilcock	240101	C.S.M.	G. Gerrard
240176	R.Q.M.S.	F. Whitehead	240029	C.Q.M.S.	J. C. O. Evans
251	C.S.M.	H. Clare	240083	Sergeant	F. Moss
531	,,	G. A. Corbett	240015	,,	A. Jones
240524	,,	E. James	240525	A/Corpl.	S. D. Clarke.

Belgian Croix de Guerre -   -   R.S.M. J. F. Wilcock.

Medal of St. George (3rd Class)   1308 Private L. Pollitt.

,,   ,,   (4th Class)   1787   ,,   H. Brooke.

Medaille D'Honeur with Swords
 in Bronze -   -   -   -   240600   ,,   J. Maddocks.

HONOURS AND AWARDS.

MENTIONED IN DISPATCHES.

5587	R.S.M.	J. F. Wilcock, M.S.M.	1573	Sergeant	A. Jones, M.S.M.
203	R.Q.M.S.	H. Holt	15667	"	W. J. Gilberts
240176	R.Q.M.S.	F. Whitehead, M.S.M.	240124	"	G. H. Ogden, M.M.
251	C.S.M.	H. Clare, M.S.M.	240477	"	G. Cruickshank, M.M.
531	"	G. A. Corbett, M.S.M.	241839	A/Sergt.	G. E. King
1647	"	H. Sweeney	15598	Corporal	C. Flynn
2268	"	J. E. Boyle	1874	L/Corpl.	A. H. Hawkesford
15602	Sergeant	S. Davies, M.M.	2048	Private	S. Hayes
2236	"	W. H. Singleton	15592	"	G. Selby
1169	"	J. W. Watkinson	240600	"	J. Maddocks

The General Officer commanding the 56th Division instituted a system of presenting Divisional Cards in recognition of gallantry or good work to non-commissioned officers and men of the Division. Recipients of these Cards frequently obtained in addition decorations or mention in despatches.

DIVISIONAL CARDS.

15602	Sergeant	S. Davies, M.M.	241164	Private	W. R. Mitchell
240472	"	C. G. Hewitt, M.M.	240391	"	S. E. Atherton
240211	L/Corpl.	G. A. Passey, M.M.	240606	"	J. Royle
240208	"	S. Billington	240958	"	C. J. Doughty, M.M.
1535	Private	C. H. Paddock	240870	"	E. N. Jones
1798	"	J. Ball	45752	"	W. Henderson
240948	"	J. Bellis	243995	"	A. Bushell
240588	"	F. Morrison			

Record of Officers' Service Abroad.

COMMANDING OFFICERS.

Lt.-Col. J. E. G. Groves, C.M.G., T.D.	14/ 2/15—21/ 2/18
Major (T/Lt.-Col.) W. A. V. Churton, D.S.O., T.D.	21/ 2/18—end of War.

SECOND IN COMMAND.

Major T. L. Fennell, T.D.	14/ 2/15—24/ 5/15
Major W. A. V. Churton, D.S.O., T.D.	25/10/15—21/ 2/18
Capt. (A/Major) N. B. Ellington, M.C.	21/ 2/18—end of War.

ADJUTANTS.

Capt. J. H. Davies	14/ 2/15—24/ 4/15
Capt. L. Bengough, M.C.	24/ 4/15—22/ 1/16
Lieut. (A/Capt.) S. H. Smith	22/ 1/16—23/ 4/16
Lieut. (A/Capt.) F. Bishop	23/ 4/16—13/12/16
Lieut. (A/Capt.) J. H. Rowlands	13/12/16—31/10/17
Lieut. (A/Capt.) H. E. Ratcliffe	31/10/17— 3/ 4/18
Lieut. (A/Capt.) J. H. Rowlands	3/ 4/18— 4/ 9/18
Lieut. W. W. Arnold	4/ 9/18—17/ 9/18
Lieut. (A/Capt.) N. Armstrong	17/ 9/18—21/ 1/19
Lieut. (A/Capt.) G. Fell Milner	21/ 1/19—30/ 6/19

QUARTERMASTERS.

Capt. T. Dutton	14/ 2/15—14/ 5/15
Capt. A. Burnett	14/ 5/15—23/ 9/16
Capt. A. Blythen	23/ 9/16— 1/11/18
Capt. W. C. Cunningham (9th Royal Scots)	23/11/18—end of War.

MEDICAL OFFICERS.

Lieut. W. Rogers,	R.A.M.C.	14/ 2/15—10/ 5/15
Lieut. R. E. Lee,	,,	10/ 5/15—19/ 7/15
Capt. J. M. A. Costello, M.C.,	,,	19/ 7/15— 4/ 5/16
Capt. F. M. Byrne,	,,	4/ 5/16— 9/11/17
1/Lieut. R. J. Miller,	M.O.R.C. (U.S.A.)	9/11/17— 4/ 9/18
Capt. G. R. Curl,	,, ,,	4/ 9/18—end of War.

CHAPLAINS.

Rev. F. D. Wilkinson	... 10/ 8/17— 5/ 9/17
Rev. F. L. Sheppard	... 29/ 4/18—end of War.

COMPANY COMMANDERS.

* "A" Company.

Major H. Watts	... 14/ 2/15—16/ 4/15
Lieut. S. H. Smith	... 16/ 4/15—21/ 4/15
Capt. J. H. Davies	... 21/ 4/15— 7/ 6/16
Capt. C. A. Price	... 7/ 6/16— 2/ 7/16
Capt. E. J. Bairstow	... 2/ 7/16—11/11/16
Lieut. (A/Capt.) J. H. Rowlands	... 11/11/16—13/12/16
2nd Lieut. N. P. Sandiford	... 13/12/16— 6/ 1/17
Lieut. (A/Capt.) E. S. Heron	... 6/ 1/17—28/ 2/17
Capt. E. J. Bairstow	... 28/ 2/17—26/ 4/17
Lieut. (A/Capt.) E. S. Heron	... 26/ 4/17—21/ 2/18

"D" Company.

Capt. N. B. Ellington	... 14/ 2/15—23/11/15
Lieut. S. P. Gamon	... 23/11/15— 4/ 2/16
Capt. E. S. Bourne	... 4/ 2/16— 4/ 4/16
Capt. O. Johnson, M.C.	... 4/ 4/16— 1/11/17
Lieut. (A/Capt.) H. W. Glendinning	... 1/11/17— 9/12/17
Capt. H. L. Churton	... 9/12/17—21/ 2/18

* On the Battalion being formed on a Three Company Establishment, "A" Company was split up and "D" Company was renamed "A."

Capt. H. L. Churton	... 21/ 2/18—13/ 5/18
Capt. O. Johnson, M.C.	... 13/ 5/18—18/ 8/18
Capt. E. J. Bairstow	... 18/ 8/18—end of War.

"B" Company.

Capt. W. A. V. Churton	... 14/ 2/15—18/10/15
Capt. E. J. Bairstow	... 18/10/15—11/ 2/16
Capt. G. Hatt-Cook	... 11/ 2/16—29/ 4/16
Capt. H. Caldecutt	... 29/ 4/16—17/ 7/16
Lieut. (A/Capt.) T. L. C. Heald	... 17/ 7/16—30/ 7/16

"B" Company—*Continued.*

Capt. H. N. Hignett	30/ 7/16—21/ 9/16
Lieut. (A/Capt.) J. D. Salmon	21/ 9/16— 4/ 1/17
Capt. N. B. Ellington	4/ 1/17—21/ 2/18
Lieut. (A/Capt.) E. S. Heron	21/ 2/18—28/ 3/18
Lieut. (A/Capt.) J. D. Salmon, M.C.	28/ 3/18—end of War.

"C" Company.

Capt. C. A. Price	14/ 2/15—15/ 3/15
Capt. G. W. C. Hartley	15/ 3/15— 3/ 5/16
Capt. E. M. Dixon	3/ 5/16—16/ 9/16
Lieut. (A/Capt.) T. L. C. Heald	16/ 9/16—22/10/16
Lieut. (A/Capt.) A. H. Jolliffe	22/10/16—10/12/16
Capt. G. W. C. Hartley	10/12/16— 3/ 1/17
Lieut. (A/Capt.) J. B. Armitage	3/ 1/17—16/ 5/17
Lieut. (A/Capt.) A. H. Jolliffe, M.C.	16/ 5/17—end of War.

NOTE—The dates given are actual dates and not those appearing in the Gazette or Part II Orders.

Roll of Officers who Served Overseas with the Battalion.

* Came out with Unit.	W. Wounded.
R.J. Rejoined Battalion.	K. Killed.
D.Z. Left Unit for Demobilization.	d. Died.

	Date of Joining Unit in France.	Remarks.
Abraham, E. W., Lieut.	11/8/16	To A.P.M., 56th Division, 3/8/17. D.Z. 6/2/19.
Allmand, A. J. (M.C.), Lieut.	26/7/15	To 3rd Army H.Q. 29/8/15.
Anderson, T. M., 2nd Lieut.	22/9/18	To 1/7th Ches. Regiment 8/3/19.
Andrews, E. J., "	26/6/16	W. 1/7/16 to England.
Armitage, J. B., Capt.	17/10/16	K. 17/5/17.
Armistead, W. K., Lieut.	11/8/16	W. 2/10/16 to England.
Armstrong, N., "	21/9/16	Adjutant 17/9/18. D.Z. 21/1/19.
Arnold, W. W., "	11/9/16	D.Z. 2/4/19.
Arthur, G. S., 2nd Lieut.	5/6/16	K. 1/7/16.
Ashworth, F. E., Lieut.	27/9/16	W. 8/5/17. To England 9/1/18. R.J. 9/10/18. D.Z. 17/2/19.
*Bairstow, E. J., Capt.	14/2/15	Adjutant, 56th Divisional School, 11/11/16. R.J. 28/2/17. VII. Corps School 26/4/17 to 3rd Army School Staff 13/11/17. R.J. 20/8/18. D.Z. 16/3/19.
Bass, P. B., Lieut.	4/5/15	K. 1/7/16.
Bean, T. W., 2nd Lieut.	5/7/17	To England 4/11/17 (Medical).
Beith, A. E., "	19/10/16	To 13th Ches. Regiment 30/10/16.
Bengough, L. (M.C.), Capt.	24/4/15	Adjutant. To 15th R. Warwick Regiment 22/1/16.
Birch, A. L., Lieut.	18/12/16	Inst. 56th Division Depôt 15/5/17. XIII. Corps Reinforcement Camp 7/12/17. D.Z. 2/1/19.

ROLL OF OFFICERS WHO SERVED OVERSEAS WITH THE BATTALION.

	Date of Joining Unit in France.	Remarks.
Birch, W. L., 2nd Lieut.	5/ 7/17	To 1/6th Ches. Regiment 2/9/17.
*Bishop, F. (M.C.), Capt.	14/ 2/15	Adjutant 29/8/16. General Staff 6/11/17. d. 21/2/19.
Blythen, A., Capt. Q..M.	23/ 9/16	England 1/11/18 (Medical).
Bourne, E. S., Capt.	8/ 8/15	To A.D.R.T. 4/4/16.
Breach, G. T., Lieut.	13/ 3/17	To 1/7 Ches. Regiment 8/3/19.
Breeze, J. E., ,,	25/ 4/18	To ,, ,, ,, ,,
Brunner, G. H., Capt.	24/ 6/18	To 56th Div. 7/7/18. D.Z. 27/1/19.
Bullock, C. W., 2nd Lieut.	10/ 9/16	To 13th Ches. Regiment 30/10/16.
*Burnett, A., Capt.	14/ 2/15	A.P.M. Tank Corps 11/10/17.
Burt, H. S., 2nd Lieut.	13/ 3/17	W. 15/8/17 to England.
Byrne, F. M., Capt.	2/ 5/16	R.A.M.C. to England 29/9/17 (Medical).
*Caldecutt, H., Capt.	14/ 2/15	To Base 1/10/16.
Capper, L. A., 2nd Lieut.	25/ 4/18	To 1/6th Ches. Regiment 16/7/18.
Carbury, A. V., ,,	21/ 1/18	To England 18/7/18 for M.G.C.
Carswell, H., ,,	10/10/16	W. 2/5/17 to England.
Chidley, E. C., ,,	24/ 1/18	To England 6/9/18 (Medical).
Church, F. S., ,,	24/ 1/18	D.Z. 2/4/19.
*Churton, H. L., Capt.	14/ 2/15	England 3/3/15 (Medical). R.J. 23/3/16. England 19/11/16. R.J. 15/11/17. W. 3/10/18 to England.
*Churton, W. A. V., (D.S.O., T.D.) Major (T/Lt.-Col.)	14/ 2/15	Took command 21/2/18, Cadre 11/6/19
Clemence, S., Lieut.	26/ 6/16	W. 16/9/16 to England.
Cook, A. E. W., 2nd Lieut.	5/ 7/17	To 1/6th Ches. Regiment 2/9/17.
Cook, T. R., Lieut.	24/ 1/18	D.Z. 27/1/19.
Corran, H., 2nd Lieut.	11/ 8/16	England 9/10/16 (Medical)
Costello, T. M. A., Capt.	19/ 7/15	R.A.M.C. to Field Ambulance 4/5/16.
Coventry, E. A., Lieut.	28/ 5/17	28/4/18 to England accidentally injured.
*Cowap, A. H., Capt.	14/ 2/15	To England 28/8/15.
*Crick, L. G. M., Lieut.	14/ 2/15	To England 12/3/15 (Medical).

Officers of "B" Company,
Dainville, 1918.

2/Lt. A. V. Carbury.   Lt. G. T. Breach.   Lt. E. L. Moore.
Capt. E. M. Dixon   Capt. J. D. Salmon, M.C.   Lt. J. H. L. Gibson.

Officers of "C" Company,
1918.

Lt. F. S. Church. Lt. A. B. Smith. Lt. H. R. Disley.
Capt. H. W. Glendinning. Capt. A. H. Jolliffe, M.C. Lt. F. J L. Roberts.

ROLL OF OFFICERS WHO SERVED OVERSEAS WITH THE BATTALION.

Name	Date of Joining Unit in France.	Remarks.
Cunningham, W. C., Capt. Q.M.	23/11/18	Attached from 9th Royal Scots Cadre 11/6/19.
Curl, G. R., Capt.	5/9/18	M.O.R.C. (U.S.A.).
Davenport, F. E., Lieut.	13/3/17	W. 1/12/17, to England.
Davies, E. W. P., 2nd Lieut.	26/10/16	To England 4/1/17.
Davies, F. A., „	30/5/16	K. 1/7/16.
*Davies, H. F., „	14/2/15	K. 3/7/15.
*Davies, J. H. (O.B.E.), Major	14/2/15	To Kite Balloon Section 7/6/16
Davies, J. S., 2nd Lieut.	26/7/15	To Y 56 T.M.B. 24/5/16 W. 29/6/16 to England.
Davies, W. E., „	21/7/15	K. 29/1/16.
Dingley, W. L., „	26/6/16	To R.F.C. 3/9/16.
Disley, H. R., Lieut.	17/9/17	DZ. 12/1/19.
*Dixon, E. M., Capt.	14/2/15	W. 15/4/15 to England, R.J. 13/2/16, W. 16/9/16 to England R.J. 7/5/18, D.Z. 25/1/19.
Drummond-Fraser, V.M., 2nd Lieut.	30/4/15	K. 3/6/15.
Dunkley, D.P., 2nd Lieut.	20/10/16	To 13th Ches. Regiment 30/10/16.
*Dutton, T. Capt. Q.M.	14/2/15	To England 16/5/15 (Medical).
Edwards, J. K., Lieut.	22/9/18	Died 28/10/18.
*Ellington, N. B. (M.C.), Capt.	14/2/15	To England for M.G.C. 23/11/15, R.J. from 11th Ches. Regiment 4/1/17, 2nd i/c 21/2/18, D.Z. 16/3/19.
*Evans, L., Lieut.	14/2/15	England 20/3/15 (Medical).
*Fennell, T. L. (T.D.), Major	14/2/15	To England 24/5/15 (Medical).
Ffoulkes, T. O. M., 2nd Lieut.	17/1/16	To England 19/8/16 (Medical).
Frater, J. G., 2nd Lieut.	11/8/16	W. 21/9/16 to England.
*Freeth, F. A. (O.B.E.), Capt.	14/2/15	To England for Munitions 25/3/15.
*Gamon, S. P., Capt.	15/2/15	To R.F.C. 10/5/16, accidentally killed 23/3/18.
Gibson, J. H. L., Lieut.	8/10/16	To 1/7th Ches. Regiment 8/3/19.
Gledhill, G., 2nd Lieut.	19/4/15	W. 11/5/15 to England.

ROLL OF OFFICERS WHO SERVED OVERSEAS WITH THE BATTALION.

	Date of Joining Unit in France.	Remarks.
Gledsdale, J., 2nd Lieut.	6/ 6/16	To 1st Ches. Regiment 26/6/16.
Glendinning, H. W., Capt.	30/ 4/15	To England 13/7/15, R.J. 16/3/16 W. 19/9/16 to England, R.J. 21/9/17, D.Z. 4/1/19.
Gordon, H., 2nd Lieut	8/10/16	To 13th Ches. Regiment 30/10/16
Gregg, B. H., Lieut.	3/ 4/15	To England 19/7/17, R.J. 31/12/18 D.Z. 18/5/19.
Greenhow, R.Y.W., Lieut.	25/ 8/18	To 1/7th Ches. Regiment 8/3/19.
*Groves, J.E.G. (C.M.G.),T.D., Lieut. Col.	14/ 2/15	To England 18/2/18 (Medical).
Hardman, L., 2nd Lieut.	5/ 7/17	To 1/6th Ches. Regiment 2/9/17.
Harper, S. A., „	6/ 6/16	To 13th Ches. Regiment 20/6/16.
Harrington, W., „	19/10/16	To 13th Ches. Regiment 30/10/16.
*Hartley, G. W. C., Capt.	14/ 2/15	To 56th Div. 4/9/16 R.J. 10/12/16 to 56th Div. 3/1/17, D.Z. 2/3/19.
Hatt-Cook, G., Capt.	6/ 8/15	To St. Omer 29/4/16.
*Heald, T. L. C. (M.C.), Capt.	14/ 2/15	To 56th Division, 22/10/16, W. 13/4/17 to England, R.J. 3/9/17. To General Staff 14/5/18.
Heron, A. P. S., 2nd Lieut	21/10/16	To 13th Ches. Regiment 30/10/16.
Heron, E. S., Capt.	21/ 7/15	K. 28/3/18.
*Hignett, H. N., Capt.	14/ 2/15	W. 21/9/16 to England.
Hime, A. N. V., 2nd Lieut.	16/ 1/16	To England 6/2/16 (Medical).
*Hodgkin, A. E. (M.C.), Capt.	14/ 2/15	W. 19/ 7/15 to England.
Holmes, W. B., 2nd Lieut.	5/ 7/17	To 1/6th Ches. Regiment 2/9/17.
*Holmstrom, C. N., Lieut.	14/ 2/15	W. 10/5/15 to England.
Hutcheson, B. L., 2nd Lieut.	3/ 7/15	R.A.M.C. Temporarily attached.
Johnson, E., 2nd Lieut.	22/ 9/18	To England 4/11/18 (Medical).
*Johnson, C. (M.B.E.), Capt.	14/ 2/15	W. 18/3/15 to England.
*Johnson, O. (M.C.), Capt.	14/ 2/15	To England 1/11/17. R.J. 13/5/18 to R.A.F. 18/8/18.
Jolliffe, A. H. (M.C.), Lieut.	1/ 4/15	W. 27/4/15 to England. R.J. 16/3/16. D.Z. 26/1/19.
Kendal, N., 2nd Lieut.	11/ 8/16	W. 21/9/16 to England.

ROLL OF OFFICERS WHO SERVED OVERSEAS WITH THE BATTALION.

	Date of Joining Unit in France.	Remarks.
Lang, C. H., 2nd Lieut.	17/ 9/17	W. 1/12/17 to England.
Lang, J., Lieut.	7/11/15	R.A.M.C. temporarily attached.
Laugharne, O. K. S., Lieut.	21/ 7/15	W. 16/6/16. R.J. 4/7/16. D.Z. 25/1/19.
Lawrence, H. J., 2nd Lieut.	22/10/16	To 13th Welch Regiment 21/12/16.
Lee, R. E., Lieut.	10/ 5/15	R.A.M.C. to 14th Field Ambulance 19/7/15.
Leigh, H. R., Lieut.	3/ 4/15	W. 1/7/16 to England.
Leigh, W. R., „	22/ 4/17	W. 26/11/17 to England.
Lisle, A. C., „	3/ 6/17	D.Z., 14/4/19.
Marsden, G. D., 2nd Lieut.	19/ 8/17	To 1/6th Ches. Regiment 2/9/17.
McEvoy, W., Lieut.	9/10/16	D.Z. 2/2/19.
*McGowan, G. (M.C.), Lieut.	14/ 2/15	To 30th Division Signal Company 28/11/15.
McKay, A. A., Lieut.	9/10/16	To England 2/6/17.
Mead, C. J., „	9/10/16	To England 20/11/18 (Medical).
Miller, R. J., „	9/11/17	M.O.R.C. (U.S.A.), W. 4/9/18 to England.
Milner, G. F., „	11/ 8/16	To England 23/2/17. R.J. 24/6/18. Adjutant 21/1/19. Cadre 11/6/19.
Monk-Jones, A., Lieut.	22/ 1/18	D.Z. 20/1/19.
Moore, E. L., „	11/ 8/16	D.Z. 28/1/19.
Morgan, E. B., „	3/ 4/15	W. 2/7/15 to England. R.J. 11/4/16. To England 15/8/16.
Newport, Gwilt R. J., Lieut.	18/12/16	To England 29/4/18.
Newton, F., 2nd Lieut.	5/ 7/17	K. 15/8/17.
*Price, C. A., Capt.	14/ 2/15	To England 15/3/15. R.J. 9/3/16. To England 12/7/16 (Medical).
Proctor, F.G., 2nd Lieut.	19/ 8/17	To 1/6th Ches. Regiment 2/9/17.
Ratcliffe, H. E., Lieut.	21/ 7/15	Adjutant 31/10/17. To Base 19/10/18.
Rees, K. D., Lieut.	17/10/16	Died of wounds 29/8/17.
Roberts, A. G., 2nd Lieut.	1/ 9/18	D.Z. 15/1/19.
Roberts, F. J. L., Lieut.	20/ 5/17	To 206 P.O.W. Company 9/3/19.

ROLL OF OFFICERS WHO SERVED OVERSEAS WITH THE BATTALION.

	Date of Joining Unit in France.	Remarks.
*Rogers, W., Capt.	14/ 2/15	R.A.M.C. W. 10/5/15 to England.
Rowlands, J. H., Capt.	6/ 8/15	Adjutant 13/12/16. W. 4/9/18 to England.
Russell, F. T., 2nd Lieut.	17/ 9/17	To England 17/ 9/18.
Sandford, G. C., 2nd Lieut.	9/10/18	To 1/7th Ches. Regiment 8/3/19.
Sandiford, N. P., "	12/ 9/16	Died of wounds 3/4/17.
Salmon, J. D. (M.C.), Lieut.	26/ 7/15	W. 10/10/15 to England. R.J. 30/5/16. D.Z. 29/1/19.
Schofield, L. D., 2nd Lieut.	10/10/16	To R.F.C. 6/1/17.
Scott, C. T., "	18/12/16	To 1/6th Ches. Regiment 2/9/17.
Sheppard, F. L., Rev.	29/ 4/18	Attached.
Simpson, E. F., 2nd Lieut.	20/ 5/17	W. 10/4/18 to England.
Simpson, H. C. H., "	15/ 1/16	W. 1/7/16 to England.
Smallwood, R. "	18/12/16	K. 18/4/17.
Smith, A. B., Lieut.	3/ 6/17	D.Z. 3/2/19.
*Smith, S. H. (M.C.), Lieut.	14/2 /15	Adjutant 22/1/16. To General Staff 2/9/16.
Smith, W. F., 2nd Lieut.	26/ 6/16	Died of wounds 28/9/16.
Snape, C. R., "	16/10/16	To 13th Ches. Regiment 30/10/16.
Spicer, R. S., Lieut.	5/ 6/16	To 1/7th Ches. Regiment 8/3/19.
Standish, K. N., Lieut.	26/ 6/16	D. Z. 2/4/19.
Stott, F., "	10/ 8/15	To M.G.C. 28/12/15.
Thomas, H. W., 2nd Lieut.	8/10/16	To 13th Ches. Regiment 30/10/16.
Vernon, F. T. "	26/ 7/15	K. 30/8/15.
Vernon, W., Capt.	8/ 8/15	To England 15/1/16.
*Walker, B. S., 2nd Lieut.	14/ 2/15	K. 9/5/15.
Walker, J. L., Lieut.	22/ 4/17	D.Z. 1/2/19.
Warrilow, O. J., 2nd Lieut.	5/ 7/17	To 1/6th Ches. Regiment 2/9/17.
*Watts, H. (O.B.E., T.D.), Major	14/ 2/15	To England 3/5/15 (Medical).
Welch, C. T. 2nd Lieut.	15/ 1/16	To England 6/5/16 (Medical).
West, F. T. "	8/10/16	To 13th Ches. Regiment 30/10/16.
Williams, G. H. (M.C.) Lieut.	13/ 3/17	DZ 21/12/18.
Wilkinson, F. D., Rev.	10/ 8/17	Attached.
Wyman, B., Lieut.	10/ 5/15	To Special Brigade R.E. 17/5/.16

Location Table of Head Quarters.

Place.	Arrived.	Departed.
Havre	15/ 2/15	17/ 2/15
Bailleul	18/ 2/15	19/ 2/15
Neuve Eglise	19/ 2/15	23/ 3/15
Kemmel	23/ 3/15	24/ 3/15
Locre (Rear H.Q.)	24/ 3/15	5/ 4/15
Hutments near Ouderdom	5/ 4/15	7/ 4/15
Cavalry Barracks, Ypres (Rear H.Q.)	7/ 4/15	15/ 4/15
Bleach Works, Kruisstraat (Rear H.Q.)	15/ 4/15	30/ 4/15
In Bivouac, Kruisstraat (Rear H.Q.)	30/ 4/15	9/ 5/15
In Bivouac, Vlamertinghe (Rear H.Q.)	9/ 5/15	11/ 5/15
In Bivouac, Dickebusch	11/ 5/15	23/ 5/15
Boeschepe	24/ 5/15	31/ 5/15
In Bivouac, Dickebusch (Rear H.Q.)	31/ 5/15	1/ 6/15
In Bivouac, Ouderdom (Rear H.Q.)	1/ 6/15	17/ 6/15
In Bivouac, Dickebusch Rear H.Q.)	17/ 6/15	1/ 7/15
In Bivouac, Ouderdom (Rear H.Q.)	1/ 7/15	8/ 7/15
In Bivouac, Dickebusch (Rear H.Q.)	8/ 7/15	17/ 7/15
In Bivouac, Ouderdom (Rear H.Q.)	17/ 7/15	24/ 7/15
Reninghelst	24/ 7/15	25/ 7/15
Eecke	26/ 7/15	1/ 8/15
Daours	1/ 8/15	4/ 8/15
Treux	4/ 8/15	8/ 8/15
Suzanne (Rear H.Q.)	9/ 8/15	29/11/15
Bray	29/11/15	29/ 1/16
Bray (Battalion Shelters)	29/ 1/16	2/ 2/16
Corbie	2/ 2/16	6/ 2/16
Saint Gratien	6/ 2/16	12/ 2/16
Breilly	12/ 2/16	13/ 2/16
Hallencourt	13/ 2/16	27/ 2/16
Domart-en-Ponthieu	27/ 2/16	12/ 3/16
Authieule	12/ 3/16	15/ 3/16
Grand Rullecourt	15/ 3/16	6/ 5/16
Souastre	6/ 5/16	20/ 8/16
Doullens	20/ 8/16	22/ 8/16
Hiermont	22/ 8/16	23/ 8/16

LOCATION TABLE OF HEAD QUARTERS.

Place.		Arrived.	Departed.
St. Riquier		23/ 8/16	4/ 9/16
Corbie		4/ 9/16	6/ 9/16
Citadel	⎫	6/ 9/16	7/ 9/16
Contour Wood	⎪	7/ 9/16	14/ 9/16
Bois De Favière	⎬ Somme.	14/ 9/16	27/ 9/16
Sandpits, Meaulte	⎪	27/ 9/16	30/ 9/16
S. of Montauban	⎪	30/ 9/16	10/10/16
Citadel	⎭	10/10/16	15/10/16
Condé		16/10/16	21/10/16
Hallencourt		21/10/16	24/10/16
Cornet-Malo		25/10/16	28/10/16
Laventie		28/10/16	4/ 3/17
Haute Rue near Merville		4/ 3/17	5/ 3/17
Arras		5/ 3/17	8/ 4/17
Trenches near Agny		8/ 4/17	17/ 4/17
Dug-outs near Achicourt		17/ 4/17	19/ 4/17
Wailly		19/ 4/17	20/ 4/17
Souastre		20/ 4/17	26/ 4/17
Talavera Camp near Agnez Les Duisans		26/ 4/17	28/ 4/17
Arras		28/ 4/17	26/ 5/17
Gouves		26/ 5/17	11/ 6/17
In Bivouac, Telegraph Hill		11/ 6/17	3/ 7/17
Gouy		3/ 7/17	4/ 7/17
Grand Rullecourt		4/ 7/17	22/ 7/17
Bouque Maison		22/ 7/17	23/ 7/17
Longuenesse		24/ 7/17	24/ 7/17
Ganspette		24/ 7/17	6/ 8/17
Connaught Camp, Wippenhoek		6/ 8/17	12/ 8/17
Ottawa Camp, Ouderdom		12/ 8/17	14/ 8/17
Chateau Segard, Ypres		14/ 8/17	18/ 8/17
Connaught Camp, Wippenhoek		18/ 8/17	26/ 8/17
Ouest Mont		26/ 8/17	30/ 8/17
In Bivouac near Bapaume		31/ 8/17	4/ 9/17
Huts near Haplincourt		4/ 9/17	22/ 9/17
Huts near Lebucquiere		22/ 9/17	30/11/17
Huts near Fremicourt		30/11/17	3/12/17
Dainville		3/12/17	5/12/17
St. Aubin		5/12/17	7/12/17
Aubrey Camp near Roclincourt		7/12/17	21/12/17
St. Catherine		21/12/17	9/ 1/18

LOCATION TABLE OF HEAD QUARTERS.

Place.	Arrived.	Departed.
Bailleul aux Cornailles	9/ 1/18	10/ 2/18
St. Catherine	10/ 2/18	31/ 3/18
Estree Cauchy	31/ 3/18	6/ 4/18
St. Aubin	6/ 4/18	7/ 4/18
Dainville (Rear H.Q.)	7/ 4/18	11/ 4/18
Wagnonlieu (Rear H.Q.)	11/ 4/18	14/ 4/18
Wanquetin (Rear H.Q.)	14/ 4/18	22/ 6/18
Arras, Rue des Capucins	22/ 6/18	13/ 7/18
Hauteville	13/ 7/18	14/ 7/18
Gouy-en-Ternois	14/ 7/18	15/ 7/18
Averdoingt	15/ 7/18	18/ 7/18
Estree Cauchy	18/ 7/18	1/ 8/18
Arras, Rue de Capucins	1/ 8/18	16/ 8/18
Beaufort	16/ 8/18	21/ 8/18
La Bazeque Farm	21/ 8/18	23/ 8/18
Block House near Blairville	23/ 8/18	25/ 8/18
Boisleux au Mont	25/ 8/18	4/ 9/18
Croisilles	4/ 9/18	7/ 9/18
Les Fosses Farm, Arras-Cambrai Road	7/ 9/18	25/ 9/18
Trench, Dury Cross Roads	25/ 9/18	15/10/18
Maroeuil	16/10/18	31/10/18
Neuville sur L'Escaut	31/10/18	2/11/18
La Pyramide de Denain	2/11/18	4/11/18
Caumont Farm	4/11/18	5/11/18
Saultain	5/11/18	8/11/18
Sebourg	8/11/18	9/11/18
Autreppe	9/11/18	10/11/18
Athis	10/11/18	28/11/18
Spiennes	28/11/18	20/ 3/19
Jemappes	20/ 3/19	9/ 6/19
Antwerp	10/ 6/19	11/ 6/19
London	12/ 6/19	13/ 6/19
Chester	13/ 6/19	—

NOTE—The Head Quarters of the Battalion was frequently divided into Advanced and Rear Head Quarters, the latter consisting of the Transport and Quartermaster's Stores and a portion of the Orderly Room Staff.

Roll of Honour.

Roll of Honour.

OFFICERS.

	Date.	Place.
Armitage, J. B., Capt.	17/ 5/17	Guemappe
Arthur, G. S., 2nd Lieut.	1/ 7/16	Gommecourt
Bass, P. B., Lieut.	1/ 7/16	Gommecourt
Bishop, F. (M.C.) Capt.	21/ 2/19	Died
Davies, F. A., 2nd Lieut.	1/ 7/16	Gommecourt
Davies, H. F., 2nd Lieut.	3/ 7/15	Ypres
Davies, W. E., 2nd Lieut.	29/ 1/16	Lucknow Redoubt
Drummond, Fraser V.M., 2nd Lieut.	3/ 6/15	Ypres
Edwards, J. K., Lieut., 7th Ches. Regiment, attached 1/5th	28/11/18	Died
Gamon, S. P., Capt.	23/ 3/18	Attached R.F.C.
Heron, E. S., A/Capt.	28/ 3/18	Ridge Post, Vimy
Newton, F., 2nd Lieut., 4th Ches. Regiment, attached 1/5th	15/ 8/17	Ypres
Rees, K. D., 2nd Lieut., 4th Ches. Regiment, attached 1/5th	29/ 8/17	Ypres
Sandiford, N. P., 2nd Lieut.	3/ 4/17	Achicourt
Scott, C. T., 2nd Lieut.	20/ 9/17	Attached 6th Ches. Regiment
Smallwood, R., 2nd Lieut.	18/ 4/17	Wancourt
Smith, W. F., 2nd Lieut.	28/ 9/16	Somme
Stott, F. G., Lieut.	11/ 7/16	Attached M.G.C.
Vernon, F. T., 2nd Lieut.	30/ 8/15	Vaux Sur Somme
Walker, B. S., 2nd Lieut.	9/ 5/15	Ypres

N.C.O's AND MEN.

			Date	Place
240081	Ackerley, C., L/Corpl.		1/ 7/16	Gommecourt
486	Adkinson, H., Private		19/ 3/15	Messines
240341	Allen, S.	,,	1/ 7/16	Gommecourt
4138	Armstrong, H.	,,	11/ 9/16	Somme
13569	Ashley, E.	,,	8/ 5/17	Wancourt
1981	Ashton, S.	,,	18/ 9/16	Somme

Roll of Honour.

			Date.		Place.
1080	Astbury, A.,	Private	8/ 4/15	...	Ypres
3705	Astbury, W.	,,	22/ 9/16	...	Somme
241175	Atherton, J.	,,	1/ 7/16	...	Gommecourt
3421	Atkin, J.	,,	1/ 7/16	...	Gommecourt
716	Baker, J.	,,	9/ 5/15	...	Ypres
241229	Ball, E. V.	,,	2/ 5/17	...	Guemappe
241424	Bancroft, H.	,,	28/ 3/18	...	Ridge Post, Vimy
1367	Barber, H.,	Corporal	11/ 6/15	...	Ypres
1701	Barton, T.,	Private	3/ 3/15	...	Messines
3502	Beatty, H.	,,	21/ 9/16	...	Somme
1303	Beesley, L. C.	,,	14/ 6/16	...	Hebuterne
2307	Bell, T.	,,	10/ 4/15	...	Ypres
4238	Bell, W.	,,	21/ 9/16	...	Somme
240073	Bellis, H.,	Sergeant	26/11/17	...	Boursies
240843	Bennett, C. H.,	Private	1/ 7/16	...	Gommecourt
241461	Bird, G.	,,	13/ 5/17	...	Wancourt
1603	Birtles, A.	,,	6/ 5/15	...	Ypres
4045	Birtwistle, W.	,,	3/10/16	...	Somme
240777	Blackburn, C.	,,	1/ 7/16	...	Gommecourt
1906	Blackburn, S.	,,	2/10/16	...	Somme
241189	Blackhurst, J.	,,	2/ 6/18	...	Arras
3818	Blackhurst, J. W.	,,	2/10/16	.	Somme
1800	Blackshaw, J.	,,	18/ 6/15	...	Ypres
1408	Blount, W.	,,	14/ 9/16	...	Somme
1605	Blythen, G.	,,	27/ 3/15	...	Kemmel
240063	Boardman, E.,	Sergeant	1/ 7/16	...	Gommecourt
240329	Boardman, J. W.,	Private	1/ 7/16	...	Gommecourt
244296	Boffey, N.	,,	1/ 5/17	...	Wancourt
57804	Bone, B. A.	,,	28/ 9/18	...	Canal du Nord
243918	Booth, W. A.	,,	26/11/17	...	Boursies
1551	Bostock, M.	,,	17/ 6/15	...	Ypres
1738	Bostock, S.	,,	28/ 4/15	...	Ypres
1988	Boulger, J. W.	,,	1/ 7/16	...	Gommecourt
240022	Bradley, A.,	Sergeant	15/10/18	...	Sauchy Cauchy
244231	Bradley, F.,	Private	8/ 5/17	...	Guemappe
3519	Bradshaw, A.	,,	11/ 9/16	...	Somme
15751	Bradshaw, G.	,,	22/ 9/16	...	Somme
1994	Brandreth, A.	,,	17/ 6/16	...	Hebuterne
1640	Brandreth, G.	,,	26/ 3/15	...	Kemmel
1493	Brazendale, S.	,,	11/ 2/16	...	(Died)

Roll of Honour.

			Date.	Place.
53081	Brocklehurst, R. B.,	Private	28/ 3/18	Ridge Post, Vimy
1736	Brocklehurst, V.	,,	1/ 7/16	Gommecourt
1787	Brookes, H.,	L./Sergt.	11/ 6/16	Hebuterne
4094	Brown, D.,	Private	1/ 7/16	Gommecourt
244318	Brown, J.	,,	6/ 4/17	Achicourt
1376	Brown, J.	,,	5/ 3/15	Neuve Eglise
268327	Brown, T.	,,	28/ 3/18	Ridge Post, Vimy
241099	Buchanan, R.	,,	1/ 7/16	Gommecourt
2184	Buckley, W.	,,	6/ 6/15	Ypres
241448	Budd, F. A.	,,	28/ 9/18	Canal du Nord
4129	Buxton, F.	,,	2/10/16	Somme
1942	Byrne, M.	,,	31/ 3/15	Kemmel
244388	Byrne, T. P.	,,	28/ 9/18	Canal du Nord
1699	Cameron, W.	,,	26/ 9/15	Maricourt
240912	Campbell, J.,	L/Corpl.	26/11/17	Boursies
52118	Carter, A. W. H.,	Private	8/ 5/17	Wancourt
241241	Carter, W.	,,	1/ 7/16	Gommecourt
1628	Cash, A.	,,	1/ 7/16	Gommecourt
2243	Cheek, F.	,,	13/ 9/16	Somme
316093	Clare, A.	,,	28/ 9/18	Canal du Nord
1779	Clarke, A.	,,	1/ 7/16	Gommecourt
3123	Clarke, A. E.	,,	1/ 7/16	Gommecourt
1527	Clifford, J.	,,	1/ 7/16	Gommecourt
1917	Cole, W.	,,	29/ 4/15	Ypres
1752	Comar, E.	,,	20/ 7/16	Fonquevillers
241287	Cook, A.	,,	16/ 8/17	Zillebeke
240559	Cook, W. H.	,,	10/ 5/17	Arras
244302	Cooke, G. W.	,,	7/ 2/17	(Died)
243966	Cooke, J. S.	,,	4/ 5/17	Tilloy
3246	Cooke, T.	,,	7/10/15	Maricourt
28270	Cookson, A.	,,	28/ 9/18	Canal du Nord
240365	Cooper, W.	,,	1/12/17	Boursies
243953	Crick, D.	,,	9/ 2/17	(Died)
2357	Crooke, F. C.	,,	5/10/16	Somme
2104	Crowther, H.	,,	9/ 7/16	Heburterne
244038	Cutler, J.	,,	5/ 3/18	Boursies
1311	Dakin, A.	,,	8/ 6/15	Ypres
240789	Davenport, H.	,,	1/ 7/16	Gommecourt
3757	Davies, D. A.	,,	21/ 9/16	Somme
240178	Davies, J.,	L/Corpl.	1/ 7/16	Gommecourt

Roll of Honour.

			Date.		Place.
243975	Davies, J. A.,	Private ...	25/ 8/18	...	Boyelles
1524	Deakin, J. W.	,, ...	8/ 9/16	...	Somme
1661	Dewhurst, A.	,, ...	4/ 4/15	...	Kemmel
1757	Donovan, J.	,, ...	19/ 7/15	...	Ypres
244063	Duckers, W. W.	,, ...	28/ 3/18	...	Vimy
1889	Dunn, O.	,, ...	27/ 3/15	...	Kemmel
240195	Dunning, J.	,, ...	1/ 5/17	...	Wancourt
3260	Dutton, H. L.	,, ...	11/ 9/16	...	Somme
241162	Dutton, N.	,, ...	1/ 7/16	...	Gommecourt
244344	Eaton, A. R., A/Sergt.	...	26/11/17	...	Boursies
1413	Edge, G., Private	...	1/ 7/16	...	Gommecourt
1126	Entwistle, H., Drummer	...	9/ 6/15	...	Ypres
244180	Everett, L.,	Private ...	22/ 9/18	...	Canal du Nord
243972	Farnworth, G.	,, ...	8/ 5/17	...	Guemappe
1534	Feeney, T.	,, ...	29/ 4/15	...	Ypres
15524	Fishbourne, T. E.	,, ...	21/ 9/16	...	Somme
240970	Fisher, J.	,, ...	16/ 6/17	...	Guemappe
240122	Fletcher, R., L/Corpl.	...	1/ 7/16	...	Gommecourt
1746	Forster, A.,	Private ...	21/ 9/16	...	Gommecourt
15653	Forster, J. W.	,, ...	8/ 9/16	...	Gommecourt
244263	Foster, G.	,, ...	8/ 5/17	...	Guemappe
15623	Fuller, G.	,, ...	7/ 9/16	...	Somme
267581	Gamson, A.	,, ...	28/ 3/18	...	Ridge Post, Vimy
241137	Gayter, H.	,, ...	1/ 7/16	...	Gommecourt
3012	Gibson, F.	,, ...	1/10/16	...	Somme
1767	Gilberts, E.	,, ...	25/ 8/15	...	Vaux Sur Somme
1439	Goff, J.	,, ...	2/10/16	...	Somme
244043	Gore, J. H.	,, ...	18/ 4/17	...	Wancourt
2728	Goulding, T.	,, ...	5/10/16	...	Somme
267001	Goulding, W.	,, ...	1/12/17	...	Boursies
1579	Green, S.	,, ...	11/ 6/15	...	Ypres
1821	Green, T.	,, ...	11/ 7/15	...	Ypres
1926	Guest, J.	,, ...	7/ 6/15	...	Ypres
3885	Hackney, P.	,, ...	5/ 9/16	...	Somme
244049	Hague, J.	,, ...	16/ 8/17	...	Ypres
240371	Hallsworth, J., L/Corpl.	...	5/ 5/18	...	Beaurains
241393	Hamlett, J., Private	...	16/ 9/18	...	Riencourt
3995	Hamman, G.	,, ...	21/ 9/16	...	Somme
2176	Harrison, C. R., Sergt.	...	23/10/15	...	Maricourt
267687	Harrold, J., Private	...	23/ 3/18	...	Ridge Post, Vimy

Roll of Honour.

			Date.	Place.
2085	Hayes, J. W.,	Private	12/ 5/15	Ypres
15677	Haywood, A.,	Corporal	1/10/16	Somme
3568	Hearn, H.,	Private	10/ 8/16	Hebuterne
1574	Heath, A. E.	„	11/ 9/16	Somme
240506	Heywood, J. L.	„	24/ 6/17	Wancourt
240123	Hinchcliffe, W.	„	1/ 7/16	Gommecourt
4026	Hinks, T.	„	21/ 9/16	Somme
240724	Hodgkinson, F.	„	4/ 9/18	Croisilles
241247	Holland, H.	„	28/ 9/18	Sauchy-Cauchy
241367	Hopley, J.	„	26/ 5/17	Guemappe
241076	Hopley, T.	„	28/ 3/18	Ridge Post, Vimy
241230	Hough, G. C.	„	27/ 3/17	Achicourt
305	Hough, H. J.	„	23/10/15	Maricourt
15635	Howard, T.	„	2/10/16	Somme
267602	Howarth, T.	„	28/ 3/18	Ridge Post, Vimy
15558	Howells, R. J.	„	8/ 9/16	Somme
2291	Hughes, A. D.,	L/Corpl.	18/ 5/15	Ypres
244370	Hunt, H.,	Private	11/ 5/17	Guemappe
1898	Jagger, A.	„	30/ 8/15	Vaux Sur Somme
1559	Jellicoe, S.	„	6/ 6/15	Ypres
44117	Johnson, W.	„	26/11/17	Boursies
244372	Jones, D.	„	20/ 5/18	Tilloy
240390	Jones, E.	„	2/ 5/17	Guemappe
1568	Jones, F. E.	„	23/ 3/15	Messines
3192	Jones, G. F.	„	1/ 7/16	Gommecourt
2350	Jones, H.	„	19/ 7/15	Ypres
1882	Jones, H.	„	30/ 5/16	Hebuterne
2351	Jones, J.	„	1/ 7/16	Gommecourt
244132	Jones, L.	„	28/ 3/18	Ridge Post, Vimy
2199	Jones, R. O.	„	24/ 3/15	Kemmel
15616	Jones, T.	„	21/ 9/16	Somme
243929	Jones, T. B.	„	27/ 1/17	Laventie
2367	Jones, T. D.	„	19/ 3/15	Messines
240546	Jones, T. P.	„	4/ 9/18	Croisilles
241364	Jones, W.	„	3/ 4/17	Achicourt
315531	Jones, W. H.	„	8/ 5/18	(Died)
2096	Jones, W. K.	„	21/ 9/16	Somme
240388	Kendall, J. A.	„	1/ 7/16	Gommecourt
2049	Kimber, H.	„	29/ 3/15	Kemmel
2050	Kinsey, W.,	A/Corpl.	1/ 7/16	Gommecourt

Roll of Honour.

			Date.		Place.
243914	Kirkpatrick, E.,	Private ...	24/ 6/17	...	Wancourt
267606	Lake, H.	,, ...	28/ 3/18	...	Ridge Post, Vimy
240273	Lamb, C.,	L/Corp. ...	6/11/18	...	(Died)
1820	Large, J.,	Corporal ...	1/ 7/16	...	Gommecourt
2503	Lawson, G. W.,	Private ...	21/ 9/16	...	Somme
266730	Lear, P.	,, ...	1/ 7/16	...	Gommecourt
240337	Lees, H.	,, ...	1/12/17	...	Boursies
1494	Leigh, P.	,, ...	1/ 4/15	...	Kemmel
241357	Leigh, W. H.	,, ...	1/ 7/16	...	Gommecourt
2041	Lindop, A.	,, ...	7/ 6/15	...	Ypres
4140	Little, J.	,, ...	3/10/16	...	Somme
1263	Lockley, T.,	Sergt. (D.C.M.)	28/12/15	...	Maricourt
3659	Lowe, L.,	Private ...	8/ 9/16	...	Somme
243977	Mallalieu, S.	,, ...	10/ 5/17	...	Guemappe
2072	Manley, A.	,, ...	10/ 4/15	...	Ypres
1260	Manton, F.,	L/Corpl. ...	9/ 9/16	...	Somme
240141	Martin, J.,	Private ...	1/ 7/16	...	Gommecourt
4147	Martin, W.	,, ...	21/ 9/16	...	Somme
1564	Mattimore, L.	,, ...	1/ 7/16	...	Gommecourt
2384	Maynard, S.	,, ...	7/ 7/15	...	Ypres
241915	McFeat, A. H.	,, ...	17/ 2/18	...	Vimy
241370	Meacock, A. T.	,, ...	18/ 4/17	...	Wancourt
2158	Meredith, F.	,, ...	24/ 4/15	...	Ypres
1904	Miller, A.	,, ...	17/ 6/15	...	Ypres
2030	Mills, G.,	L/Corpl. ...	17/ 6/15	...	Ypres
240184	Minshall, J.,	Private ...	1/ 7/16	...	Gommecourt
2172	Molyneux, G. H.	,, ...	25/ 4/15	...	Ypres
241170	Moores, J.	,, ...	1/ 7/16	...	Gommecourt
1162	Morgan, F.	,, ...	2/ 5/15	...	Ypres
15566	Morris, H. G.	,, ...	8/ 9/16	...	Somme
15644	Mounsey, J. S.	,, ...	1/10/16	...	Somme
240736	Mugan, J.	,, ...	1/ 7/16	...	Gommecourt
2305	Naylor, H.,	Sergeant ...	21/ 9/16	...	Somme
1420	Nicholas, O.,	Private ...	20/ 4/15	...	Ypres
1675	Nield, J.	,, ...	12/11/15	...	(Died)
1197	Norbury, F.,	L/Sergt. ...	6/ 3/15	...	Messines
241029	Nuttall, S. V.,	Private ...	16/ 8/17	...	Ypres
1474	Oates, J. A.	,, ...	19/ 3/15	...	Messines
1686	Oldham, A. E.,	Sergt. ...	8/ 9/16	...	Somme
3345	Orme, J. E.,	Private ...	10/ 8/16	...	Hebuterne

			Date.	Place.
241920	Orr, J.,	Private ...	24/ 6/17 ...	Wancourt
241269	Owens, J. E.	,, ...	2/ 6/18 ...	Vimy
1393	Pagett, W. H.	,, ...	16/ 6/15 ...	Ypres
244134	Parker, F. H.	,, ...	28/ 3/18 ...	Ridge Post, Vimy
15591	Parker, J. H.	,, ...	1/10/16 ...	Somme
1651	Parker, W.	,, ...	1/ 7/16 ...	Gommecourt
2091	Parsonage, R.	,, ...	27/ 3/15 ...	Kemmel
821	Partin, G., Sergeant	...	26/ 3/15 ...	(Died)
45798	Pate, H., Private	...	1/12/17 ...	Boursies
2752	Pate, W. C.	,, ...	21/ 9/16 ...	Somme
315296	Pearson, A.	,, ...	28/ 3/18 ...	Vimy
240518	Peers, F., L/Sergt.	...	8/ 5/17 ...	Wancourt
2297	Peirce, P. H., Sergeant	...	1/ 7/16 ...	Gommecourt
241328	Pemberton, T., Private	...	24/ 6/17 ...	Wancourt
3723	Percival, G.,	,, ...	10/ 8/16 ...	Hebuterne
2430	Perry, N. R.	,, ...	1/ 7/16 ...	Gommecourt
241128	Phillips, A.	,, ...	1/ 1/17 ...	Laventie
2506	Phillips, C.	,, ...	8/10/16 ...	Somme
243941	Pickles, W.	,, ...	9/ 5/17 ...	Guemappe
65409	Poock, F. W.	,, ...	28/ 3/18 ...	Vimy
241085	Poole, W.	,, ...	1/ 7/16 ...	Gommecourt
240321	Poole, W. M.	,, ...	13/ 5/17 ...	Wancourt
1521	Postles, H.	,, ...	27/ 3/15 ...	Kemmel
15551	Powell, G. T.	,, ...	8/ 9/16 ...	Somme
4153	Powell, J. W.	,, ...	1/10/16 ...	Somme
2355	Prandal, O.	,, ...	19/ 7/15 ...	Ypres
241284	Preece, E. A.	,, ...	9/ 5/17 ...	(Died)
2024	Pybus, H.	,, ...	23/10/15 ...	Maricourt
1434	Pye, A. E., Sergeant	...	27/ 6/16 ...	Hebuterne
1920	Rackstraw, W., Private	...	1/ 7/16 ...	Gommecourt
241037	Rafferty, J.	,, ...	19/ 4/17 ...	(Died)
3795	Rees, W. A.	,, ...	1/ 7/16 ...	Gommecourt
2251	Rhodes, H.	,, ...	28/ 4/15 ...	Ypres
267699	Ross, W.	,, ...	28/ 3/15 ...	Vimy
2108	Saunders, J. H.	,, ...	28/ 4/15 ...	Ypres
240661	Shaw, H.	,, ...	1/ 7/16 ...	Gommecourt
4102	Shaw, T.	,, ...	8/ 9/16 ...	Somme
3072	Shaw, W.	,, ...	1/ 7/16 ...	Gommecourt
3368	Shirt, J.	,, ...	1/ 7/16 ...	Gommecourt
241436	Shropshire, G.	,, ...	4/ 9/18 ...	Croisilles

Roll of Honour.

			Date.	Place.
3161	Silver, W.,	Private	1/ 7/16	Gommecourt
240801	Slater, H.	,,	13/ 5/18	Germany (P.O.W.)
1502	Sloane, J.	,,	27/ 4/15	Ypres
240805	Stephenson, W.	,,	28/ 3/18	Vimy
244280	Stockton, J.	,,	4/ 9/18	Croisilles
1711	Stonier, J.	,,	23/10/15	Maricourt
240257	Sutcliffe, H., Drummer		1/ 7/16	Gommecourt
1647	Sweeney, F., C.S.M.		22/ 9/16	Somme
241044	Tapley, H. T.,	Private	29/12/17	Boursies
3576	Tapley, S.	,,	11/ 9/16	Somme
1403	Taylor, J. T.	,,	19/ 7/15	Ypres
240583	Thomas, H., Corporal		1/ 7/16	Gommecourt
1771	Thomas, S.	,,	29/ 4/15	Ypres
803	Thornber, G.,	Private	17/10/15	Maricourt
2403	Thorpe, H.	,,	20/10/15	Maricourt
2328	Tiddy, P. E.	,,	17/ 4/15	Ypres
200832	Tippins, C. J.	,,	28/ 3/18	Ridge Post, Vimy
1657	Turner, F.	,,	1/ 7/16	Gommecourt
243917	Turnock, W.	,,	24/ 6/17	Wancourt
3320	Wakefield, J. W.	,,	1/ 7/16	Gommecourt
240094	Walker, F.	,,	1/ 7/16	Gommecourt
240591	Walker, F.	,,	1/ 7/16	Gommecourt
430	Walker, J. W., Corporal		18/ 8/15	Vaux Sur Somme
244135	Walker, R. W. A., Private		17/ 5/17	Guemappe
244374	Walsh, S.	,,	28/ 3/18	Vimy
2153	Ward, W.	,,	27/ 3/15	Kemmel
2113	Warnock, A., C.S.M.		2/ 5/15	(Died)
4218	Watkinson, W. J., Private		1/ 7/16	Gommecourt
1786	Wharton, E., Corporal		27/ 6/16	Hebuterne
2667	White, F.,	Private	1/ 7/16	Gommecourt
1382	White, G. A.	,,	22/ 8/15	Maricourt
240726	White, J. T.	,,	4/ 4/17	Arras
2255	Whitfield, H.	,,	22/ 4/15	Ypres
3015	Whitney, H. D.	,,	1/ 7/16	Gommecourt
1720	Wilcox, W. J.	,,	11/ 8/16	Fonquevillers
241205	Wilding, P.	,,	24/ 6/17	Wancourt
1436	Wilkinson, J. T., Sergt.		21/ 9/16	Somme
4280	Williams, A. J., Private		21/ 9/16	Somme
1624	Williams, C.	,,	9/ 4/15	Ypres
243945	Williams, J. S.	,,	7/ 4/17	Beaurains

Roll of Honour.

		Date.	Place.
1670	Williamson, J., A/Sergt.	10/ 4/15	Ypres
3984	Wilson, G., Private	2/10/16	Somme
2104	Wilson, P. ,,	2/ 6/15	Ypres
15545	Wood, W. G., Sergeant	9/ 9/16	Somme
244023	Worsley, J. E., Private	12/ 4/18	(Died)
1062	Yarwood, J. ,,	1/ 7/16	Gommecourt
1932	Yates, A. ,,	18/ 1/16	(Died)

NOTE.—The Dates and Places in the case of those who died of wounds shew when and where the man was wounded.

N.C.O's AND MEN (attached to other Units).

4331	Armitage, J. W., Private	2079	Jones, R., Private
4952	Bates, S. ,,	28634	King, G. E. ,,
291380	Broadhead, F., A/Corp.	241324	Lee, C. ,,
268157	Burton, H. M., Private	53090	Mason, A. ,,
2237	Fairclough, C. ,,	240814	Riley, D. P. ,,
243588	Hayes, W. ,,	291843	Roe, F. ,,
2154	Hitchen, W. Sergeant		

Summary of Casualties.

	Killed or died of Wounds.	Wounded.
OFFICERS	20	31
N.C.O'S AND MEN	306	1009

Lightning Source UK Ltd.
Milton Keynes UK
UKOW01f2315160414

230056UK00001B/39/P